Alfredo Viazzi's Italian Cooking

Alfredo Viazzi's Italian Cooking

Vintage Books
A Division of Random House
New York

First Vintage Books Edition, November 1983
Copyright © 1979 by Alfredo Viazzi
All rights reserved under International and
Pan-American Copyright Conventions. Published in
the United States by Random House, Inc., New York.
and simultaneously in Canada by Random House of
Canada Limited, Toronto. Originally published by
Random House, Inc. in 1979.

Library of Congress Cataloging in Publication Data
Viazzi, Alfredo.
Alfredo Viazzi's Italian cooking.
Includes index.
1. Cookery, Italian.
I. Title.
II. Title: Italian cooking.
TX723.V53 1983   641.5945   83-47818
ISBN 0-394-71747-3

Manufactured in the United States of America

*To Jane, with a pinch of nutmeg and
a pinch of ginger*

ABOUT FOOD AND
THE ART OF ENJOYING IT

President Thomas Jefferson was always one of my favorite Americans because of his predilection and taste for excellent food and wines. I often wonder what the answer would have been if someone had asked the author of the Declaration of Independence at his deathbed whether the "sinful feasts" (as he called his lavish banquets) were worth the $40,000 debt he was leaving. I'm sure his answer would have been: "Yes! Every penny of it!"

I would like to thank Milton Glaser, John Ferrone, Ann Gussow and the late Helen McCully for her precious friendship.

Contents

Alfredo Viazzi's Italian Cooking

Introduction

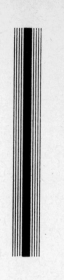

Italians are constantly discussing food, no matter what the time of day or the place, and as far back as I can remember it was the chief topic of conversation while I was growing up in Italy. When I was eight years old and going to school in Savona, one of my teachers would delight in asking us pupils what we had eaten for dinner the night before. Whenever my turn came I would always be a little embarrassed, since my answers read like a restaurant bill of fare and made the entire class laugh; Arrosto di Manzo Capriccioso, Gamberi alla Livornese, Buccelato della Sora Tina . . . as a matter of fact, these rather pompous names *did* come from a bill of fare, for the simple reason that I grew up on trattoria and restaurant food. My mother was an abominable cook, and my father, a snobbish gourmand. In order to please his palate and protect his stomach, we ate out on an average of four nights a week. On Sundays we would have our dinner sent in from that blessed Trattoria Toscana. It is not surprising, then, that I should feel so at home in the restaurant business.

The recipes in this book are organized to follow the order of an Italian menu and also the menus of my two restaurants in New York, the Trattoria da Alfredo and Tavola Calda da Alfredo. You will discover that the dishes are by no means "classic." On the contrary, they are often unorthodox. They reflect my disdain of conventional food and my efforts to keep my cooking from becoming boring, both to my patrons and to me. I believe that, *al fondo,* what makes a good chef is his inventiveness and his daring, as well as a love for food. His own personality should go into the cooking.

Not long ago a loyal patron who had just returned from a holiday in Europe said to me, "I asked for your Scaloppine Tancredi all over Italy. No one ever heard of it. How come?" Simple. Signor Tommaso Tancredi was my history teacher in the eighth grade. His name happened to come to mind while I was improvising a new dish.

Improvisation is very much a part of my style of cooking, as it is of the Italian character, and it underlines the intention to write not a classic Italian cookbook but my own—to offer a way of cooking, a style that does not come from the teachings of famous cooking schools but from what I've learned by watching and assisting my chefs. My food is prepared and cooked to taste the way I think food should taste. In this individuality,

I have very much followed in the footsteps of trattorie chefs in Italy, who alone have succeeded in creating an honest, savory manner of cooking, which is essentially improvised cooking based on traditional ideas.

In any event, there is no such thing as a *cucina classica italiana* to be found from Milano to Palermo. Italy remains a country of dialects and regional food. To my knowledge, Pellegrino Artusi, a Tuscan of the last century, came closest to standardizing the Italian cuisine in his well-conceived cookbook, *La Scienza in Cucina,* although the recipes of his own region predominate. I am a Genovese, so you might expect me to write only of the kitchen of that region. You will find, however, that the recipes range from one corner of Italy to the other. What I offer is the Italian cooking I know, as liberated from dogma as I can make it, and free of pretensions and improbable references to ancient manuscripts. My way of cooking is me.

I am happy to say that these recipes have pleased many discriminating palates, among them those of chefs Bocuse, Guérard, Vergé and Lenôtre; and of James Beard, who is also my favorite eater. The pleasure of preparing food constitutes an act of seduction. It is also showmanship—setting up a feeling, an adventure, perhaps best expressed by two older ladies who came to lunch one sunny day in June shortly after the Trattoria was opened. As they were leaving the restaurant, after a meal that they clearly relished, one of them turned, smiled at me and said, ''Ah, now we must go back to the United States.'' I hope you enjoy your visit to my Italian kitchen as much as they did.

Ingredients

ACCIUGHE/*ANCHOVIES*

I use anchovies in many recipes. I prefer Masso anchovies, a Portuguese brand packed in olive oil that can be purchased at Italian grocers. Unfortunately it is only obtainable in 14- and 28-ounce cans. Therefore, almost any of the smaller cans of imported anchovies packed in olive oil will suffice. However, avoid using the so-called cocktail anchovies, which are preserved in a strongly aromatic liquid.

Keep any leftover anchovies refrigerated in their own preserving oil, but do not keep more than a week after opening. They will get terribly salty, and the taste will change radically. Whenever you make a recipe that calls for anchovies, avoid using salt until the very end of the cooking process, when you will taste the dish to see if any is needed.

ACETO/*VINEGAR*

I always use red wine vinegar at my restaurants. I recommend the Regina brand if you can find it; otherwise, Progresso or Pastene will do. I am not fond of flavored vinegar, aside from some white wine vinegars in which tarragon is preserved. These should be used sparingly because of the strong flavor.

BACON AND PANCETTA

I use bacon only in spinach salad. It should be lean, smoked bacon. Elsewhere in my recipes I use pancetta. This is a type of Italian bacon that resembles prosciutto. It is processed differently from American bacon, cured in salt and black pepper, and made up in a casing like salami. It has a more delicate flavor and is less greasy than bacon.

BURRO, OLIO D'OLIVA, OLIO DI VEGETALI/ *BUTTER, OLIVE OIL, VEGETABLE OIL*

I use more butter (lightly salted) than oil in my recipes, which is very much the custom in North Italian kitchens, since butter gives delicacy and a more subtle flavor to a dish than oil. A great many of my sauces are also made with cream, with which butter blends nicely.

I use olive oil mainly in the making of dressings for salads and other raw vegetables, and in stocks. Also, whenever a sauce requires a stronger taste, I use olive oil rather than butter. Since olive oil does not burn as easily as butter, it is preferable for sauces that require a longer cooking time. In general, olive oil rather than vegetable oil should be used whenever the oil is going to become part of the sauce served with a dish.

Vegetable oil should be used for cooking purposes, for example, in deep frying. The oil can be discarded after use or strained through a fine wire strainer, refrigerated, and used again. If used again, it should be for the same type of food.

Often I mix oil and butter in my recipes. For instance, I sauté scaloppine first in vegetable oil, discard it, and use butter in the final cooking.

For use in my restaurants, I prefer Re di Puglia olive oil. This oil can be purchased only through a restaurant supplier, but three brands I would also recommend can be purchased in retail stores. They are Sasso, Bertolli and Berio olive oils. Among the vegetable oils, I prefer Wesson.

ERBE/*HERBS*

I use herbs in a more liberal way than most chefs. I might also call it a more adventurous way. I often experiment with different combinations, especially when using fresh herbs. This gives many of my dishes the undefined taste of a bouquet of herbs rather than the specific taste of one herb, and I firmly believe the result is more interesting.

Even in preparing traditional northern Italian foods, I sometimes ignore the rules and finish off a dish to please my own palate. I think this is the privilege of any dedicated chef.

Whenever possible I use fresh herbs, especially basil, tarragon, rosemary—and particularly parsley.

FAGIOLI/*BEANS*

CRANBERRY BEANS: spotted white and dark pink. They can be obtained fresh (in season) or dry.

CANNELLINI: creamy in color; commonly found either dry or in cans.

RED KIDNEY BEANS (so named for their reddish-brown color and their shape): commonly found dry or canned.

ROMAN BEANS: creamy in color but much larger and flatter than cannellini, and resembling lima beans. They are seldom found fresh in America but can be obtained in cans.

FAVA BEANS (*marble beans*): one of the most flavorful and delicious of all the beans; can be found fresh or dry. They are a vivid green color and larger than the usual lima bean. The pod has a fuzzy texture, almost like that of a peach. This type of bean is widely served in the springtime and is eaten raw. A delicious combination is a thin slice of salame wrapped around 2 or 3 fava beans.

CECI BEANS, or chick peas: usually found dry or in cans. In the Ligurian region, a very tasty pizza is made with ceci flour mixed with water and salt. It is rolled very thin and baked in olive oil in wood-burning ovens. Ceci beans are also used in salads and soups.

Marvelous salads can be made with any of these beans and Trattoria House Dressing or an oil and vinegar dressing of your choice. Canned Italian tuna fish might be added.

FARINA DI POLENTA/*CORN MEAL*

Polenta is a versatile food that is delicious in its many uses. A staple food of the Venetians, it is also widely used in other northern regions. It is served mainly in the fall and winter.

I prefer loose farina di polenta, bought by the pound, rather than the packaged type. It is usually found in Italian grocery stores, many of which advertise whenever there is a fresh shipment. If you buy an American packaged brand of corn meal, such as Quaker, you should put it through a flour sifter before using.

There is also on the market a packaged instant polenta, mostly imported from Italy, which requires exactly 5 minutes to cook, simplifying the process. The results are satisfying enough.

FORMAGGI/*CHEESES*
Parmigiano/*Parmesan*

There are two distinct types of Parmesan cheese. One is called grana, a fairly young cheese, usually light yellow in color. It is more flaky than the Parmesan cheese used in cooking and is often eaten with fruit or served as a table cheese. The other

type of Parmesan cheese, specified in my recipes, is a more aged cheese. It is dryer, harder and a very light yellow, almost white in color. Parmesan cheese is indigenous to Emilia or Parma, although excellent Parmesan is now made in Wisconsin and in Argentina. It is best to grate Parmesan cheese just before using. I am completely opposed to grated cheese sold in jars.

Pecorino

Pecorino (derived from the Italian word for sheep, "pecora") is made from sheep's milk. In this country it is often called Romano cheese. It is sharper than Parmesan and used only with certain pasta dishes such as pesto and amatriciana. It is also mixed with Parmesan to garnish soups like pasta e fagioli. Fresh pecorino, when obtainable, can be used as a fine table cheese. Pecorino or Romano cheese is used mostly in South Italian cooking.

Ricotta

Fresh ricotta is a soft cheese with a delicate flavor. It does not keep for more than a few days. It generally comes in two different grades—whole-milk ricotta or skimmed-milk ricotta. It is used for fillings and can also be eaten by itself (like cottage cheese) with olive oil, salt and pepper added to it. Served with fresh fruit, it is a good diet dessert cheese. It is also used in many other desserts, such as cheesecake and pastries. Ricotta, too, is a cheese that is used mostly in South Italian cooking.

Mozzarella

Mozzarella is made from cow's milk and comes in three different forms: a hard type, used for filling, toppings and baked dishes; a fresh, softer type, used in many recipes or served as a table cheese; and smoked mozzarella, excellent as an appetizer and piquant in flavor. Fresh mozzarella should not be kept for more than a few days. Mozzarella, again, is used mostly in South Italian cooking.

Fontina and Fonduta

Fontina is a mild cheese, generally used as a table cheese or as a topping on baked dishes. It should not be too dark yellow in color. A slightly oily surface indicates that it is past its prime, and no longer a good eating cheese.

Fonduta is a type of fontina used for cooking. It has a softer texture and stronger flavor and smell. Both fontina and fonduta are part of North Italian cooking.

Gorgonzola

Gorgonzola cheese originates in Lombardy, in Northern Italy. It is rich, very creamy, with a strong flavor and aroma, and somewhat similar to the French Roquefort but of a finer texture. Gorgonzola should be served at the proper degree of ripeness—when the white part of the cheese is soft, almost running. There is no domestic Gorgonzola, and the imported brand that I recommend is Colombo. In buying Gorgonzola, one should watch for excessive dryness. This indicates that the wheel of cheese has been in storage too long and is therefore past its prime.

There are many uses for Gorgonzola, including one of my favorite sandwiches. It consists of fresh Italian bread split in half, buttered, then filled with a goodly amount of Gorgonzola and baked in a preheated oven of 350°F for about 6 minutes.

FUNGHI FRESCHI/*FRESH MUSHROOMS*

There are many uses for fresh mushrooms in Italian cooking. For use as a garnish or for stuffed mushrooms, select large mushrooms, making sure that the caps are not overly spotted with brown. For mushrooms to be used in sauces, buy smaller ones, which are less expensive. Before using, wash thoroughly under cold water to remove all dirt. I slice mushrooms rather thickly in my recipes. They should be cooked for only a short time in order to retain the full flavor. I never use canned or frozen mushrooms.

FUNGHI SECCHI/*DRIED MUSHROOMS*

A great many of my recipes call for imported dried mushrooms. They have a wonderful flavor and add a great deal of distinction to a dish. They should be carefully selected because a good amount of dirt is often still on them. The pieces should be rather large, since small fragments are practically unusable, and they should be of a cream and brown color, not black. Store them in the refrigerator.

To prepare, first place mushrooms in a strainer and wash under cold water until thoroughly clean. Soak the exact number of pieces you plan to use in ½ cup of lukewarm water at least 2½ hours before using. If you have cleaned the mushrooms properly beforehand, you can safely use the water after it has been strained. Do not keep mushrooms soaking for more than a day.

Most dried mushrooms come from Europe, and I prefer the Italian variety from Emilia called Borgotaro. Of course, very good dried mushrooms also come from France, Poland and other countries. Dried mushrooms are expensive because of their seasonal nature and the long process involved in picking and drying them.

NOCI/*NUTS*

Those most commonly used in Italian cooking are walnuts and pignoli. Pignoli, or pine nuts, are pale, slender, delicately flavored ovals about ½ inch long. Both walnuts and pignoli are used in stuffings and sauces.

OLIVE DI GAETA/*GAETA OLIVES*

Gaeta olives are a variety of black olives indigenous to the Campania region of Italy. They are actually reddish-purple in color and, along with Greek Kalamata olives, are the most succulent and flavorful of olives.

Gaeta olives are used mainly in cooking. When they are fresh (before being cured and bottled), they are quite bitter but are delicious with fresh bread and hard cheese. Gaeta olives are rather expensive and can be obtained in Italian grocery stores.

OLIVE VERDI/*SPANISH GREEN OLIVES*

A rather large green olive used often in salads or as a garnish, very flavorful and a bit salty.

PASTAS

AGNOLOTTI: semi-circular stuffed ravioli

CANNELLONI: 4 x 4-inch pasta sheets, stuffed and rolled

FETTUCCELLE: ribbon noodles, a little narrower than fettuccine

FETTUCCINE: ribbon noodles about ¼ inch wide

FUSILLI: short pasta twisted like a corkscrew

LASAGNE: wide, flat pasta, used for a baked dish of meats, sauce and cheese

ORECCHIETTE: "little ears"; round pasta about the size of a nickel

PENNE: tubular pasta cut on the diagonal in short lengths

PERCIATELLI: Long, hollow macaroni thicker than spaghetti

RAVIOLI (Pansoti): filled squares of pasta

RIGATONI: grooved, tubular pasta

SPAGHETTINI: finer form of spaghetti

TAGLIARINI: narrow ribbon noodles

TORTELLINI: a filled pasta twisted to form a ring

POMODORI/*TOMATOES*

The market and season permitting, I like to use fresh, well-ripened tomatoes for cooking. Otherwise, my favorite brand of canned, peeled plum tomatoes is Vitelli, from San Marzano, Italy. I like this brand best because of the consistency in the degree of ripeness of the tomatoes, the juice content and the well-balanced seasoning of basil leaves. I would also recommend Progresso and Pastene brands. There are also some excellent brands from California, Spain and Morocco. I would not recommend any brand that has had sugar added to it, and I am definitely against adding sugar when cooking tomato sauce.

TOMATO PASTE

I use a tomato paste from California, sold by my supplier. Since it is not available in retail stores, other brands that I would recommend are Contadina, Pastene and Progresso.

PROSCIUTTO

Among the several types and brands of prosciutto available in this country, I prefer Volpi and Hormel. Both brands are domestic. I personally use Volpi because I find it less stringy and salty than Hormel. For use in cooking, I definitely recommend domestic prosciutto. If you can obtain imported prosciutto, you might wish to try Danieli for a treat to serve with melon or figs, though it is very expensive.

When buying prosciutto, look to see that it does not have too much fat. If it does, have the butcher trim some of it off. The color should be pinkish red, not dark red, and it should be cut in paper-thin slices. If it has any iridescent traces in it, do not buy it. This indicates that it is about to go bad, which is also true of ham.

RISO/*RICE*

I always use imported Arborio rice, which comes from the region of Lombardy in Italy. Since it has a longer and firmer grain than any other type of rice, it maintains its texture and taste longer, when cooked properly. I use rice primarily for risotto, but I also recommend Arborio rice for fillings, soups and salads.

Although not as desirable, other types of rice can be substituted.

SALAMI

In Italy there are almost as many varieties of salami as there are of pasta. Some well-known types are Genoa, Milanese, the wonderfully flavorful finocchiona from Tuscany, sopressata from the southern regions, the salami of Varsi, from the Piedmont region, salame cotto, and the mortadella from Bologna, as well as various coppas. Although primarily eaten as appetizers or in sandwiches, many are also used in cooking, often in stuffings.

An American-made salame that I use in some of my stuffings (such as stuffed mushrooms), and that I can recommend, is available under the brand name Aldani.

SALSICCIE/*SAUSAGES*

There are a great many varieties of regional sausages in the Italian kitchen. The so-called sweet and hot sausages are from the southern regions of Italy. Lamb and cheese sausage is typical of Bari. Luganega is a very thin pork sausage from the North. Also common in the northern region is cured fresh sausage that must be boiled and cooked before eating. The best known is the Milanese cotechino. Zampino di maiale is a soft salame that must be cooked; and zampone di Bologna is actually a peasant dish of pressed meat. The casing of zampone is the skin of the pig's leg. Both zampino and zampone are usually served only in the winter.

For stuffing and sauces I use sweet sausage exclusively.

VINI/*WINES*

In cooking I generally use dry white or red California wines. I prefer robust wines. For some recipes I use a wine of more definite aroma and taste, such as Barolo or Marsala, either dry or sweet.

It is my belief that the wine used for cooking should be suitable for drinking as a table wine. One learns how to use wine in cooking by smelling or tasting, or both. It is important to know when the wine has evaporated enough and will not leave a harsh taste on the palate. The flavor of a dish can easily be ruined if the wine is not used judiciously or reduced to the proper degree.

In peasant Italian cooking, especially in the North, you often see people putting a few tablespoons of red wine directly into a piping hot bowl of soup.

Antipasti

MARINATA DI GAMBERONI E FUNGHI
Marinated Shrimp and Mushrooms

This Tuscan dish is found chiefly in the osterie or trattorie along the waterfront in the city of Livorno. It is usually offered as an appetizer or midday snack, accompanied by local wines, such as a robust Chianti, and good fresh homemade bread.

I first sampled this delicious dish many years ago at the Osteria dei Quattro Mori in Livorno and subsequently coaxed the recipe out of the proprietor's wife, who I still remember for her hysterically bright red hair and her kindness.

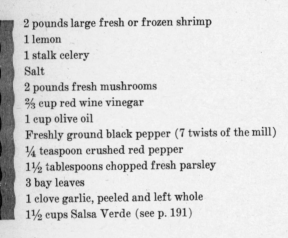

2 pounds large fresh or frozen shrimp
1 lemon
1 stalk celery
Salt
2 pounds fresh mushrooms
⅔ cup red wine vinegar
1 cup olive oil
Freshly ground black pepper (7 twists of the mill)
¼ teaspoon crushed red pepper
1½ tablespoons chopped fresh parsley
3 bay leaves
1 clove garlic, peeled and left whole
1½ cups Salsa Verde (see p. 191)

Bring a large pot of salted water to a boil. Add shrimp, the juice of the lemon and its rind, and the celery. Boil shrimp for about 3 minutes. Drain. Cool shrimp under cold running water. Shell and devein. Place in refrigerator.

Wash mushrooms well and cut in halves. Bring 1 gallon of water to a boil, add ⅓ cup vinegar and the mushrooms, and cook 15 minutes. Drain. Cool under cold running water. Drain again, and transfer to a deep glass bowl. Add the oil, remaining ⅓ cup vinegar, black pepper, red pepper, parsley, bay leaves and garlic. The marinade should cover the mushrooms completely. Marinate overnight in the refrigerator.

When ready to assemble, place the shrimp in a large salad bowl. Drain the mushrooms and mix with shrimp. Pour the salsa verde over this, and mix well. The remaining marinade can be stored in the refrigerator in a tightly closed jar, for use over boiled meats, chicken or vegetables.

Serves 6-10.

VONGOLE OREGANATE DI GAETA
Baked Clams, Gaeta Style

The reason I called this dish Vongole Oreganate di Gaeta was largely whimsical. However, there is one plausible reason for it: the *vongole* (clams) of Gaeta, a small town near Naples, are regarded as the best in Italy, their reputation being something like that of Maine lobsters.

36 medium-sized fresh clams
1½ cups unflavored bread crumbs
⅔ cup grated Parmesan cheese
¼ cup freshly chopped parsley
1 teaspoon chopped garlic
1 teaspoon oregano
½ teaspoon thyme
½ teaspoon basil
¼ cup dry sherry
Freshly ground black pepper (7 mill twists)
¾ cup olive oil
¾ cup chicken or canned consommé (see p. 42)
1 lemon, cut into wedges

Open clams (as if preparing clams on the half-shell) and save all their juice; put clams in baking pan and refrigerate.

In a large mixing bowl, combine bread crumbs, cheese, parsley, garlic, herbs, sherry, pepper, clam juice and all but 2 tablespoons of olive oil. Mix well until all ingredients are nicely moistened. Remove clams from refrigerator and cover with a layer of the mixture, being careful not to overstuff.* Add con-

---

* Leftover stuffing may be refrigerated and used later.

sommé to pan, making sure not to wet the stuffing. Drip remaining olive oil over top of each clam. Bake in preheated 350°F oven for about 15 minutes, then place pan under broiler until stuffing is well browned and crusty. Spoon the juice from the pan over each clam, and serve 6 clams per person. Serve lemon wedges with them.

Serves 6.

MELANZANE RIPIENE
Stuffed Eggplant

Eggplant is used widely in the Italian kitchen, and the treatment for stuffing varies from region to region. This recipe is prepared in the Genovese style. It can be served as an appetizer or as a main dish, accompanied by a cold, fresh string bean salad (see p. 180).

8 baby Italian eggplants
½ cup vegetable oil
½ cup beef or chicken consommé (see p. 42)
Salt
½ loaf Italian bread, coarsely broken
1 pint heavy cream (milk can also be used)
10 slices prosciutto
1 egg yolk
1 cup grated Parmesan cheese
1 tablespoon chopped parsley
Pepper to taste
Pinch nutmeg
½ cup unflavored bread crumbs

Wash eggplant under cold water. Cut off stems and bottoms, and cut in half lengthwise. Leaving shells about ¼ inch thick, scoop out pulp and set aside. Place skin side down in a baking pan. Pour ¼ cup oil and ¼ cup consommé over them, and sprinkle with salt. Set aside.

Soak bread in cream for ½ hour. Chop prosciutto into confetti-size pieces. Chop one half of the pulp finely and discard the rest. Shred the softened bread until it is almost a paste. In a mixing bowl, combine bread, egg yolk, Parmesan cheese, parsley, pepper, nutmeg, prosciutto bits and eggplant pulp. Mix well.

Now, place the eggplant shells in a preheated 350°F. oven; cook 15 minutes. Drain off liquid completely as it will have become bitter. When cooked eggplant shells have cooled, stuff with the prepared mixture. Sprinkle with bread crumbs. Pour remaining oil and consommé into a baking dish. Place stuffed eggplant side by side and bake about 15 minutes more, or until tops are golden color. Discard juice.

Serves 8.

FUNGHI FARCITI DELLA SORA ROSA
Signora Rosa's Stuffed Mushrooms

I call this dish Della Sora (Roman dialect for Signora or Mrs.) Rosa in honor of an authentic Trasteverina who owns and runs a restaurant in Vicolo Della Paglia behind Piazza di Santa Maria in Trastevere in Rome. Sora Rosa is the Anna Magnani of food and has the plumpest and sexiest hands of any restaurateur I have ever met.

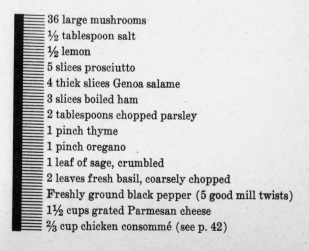

36 large mushrooms
½ tablespoon salt
½ lemon
5 slices prosciutto
4 thick slices Genoa salame
3 slices boiled ham
2 tablespoons chopped parsley
1 pinch thyme
1 pinch oregano
1 leaf of sage, crumbled
2 leaves fresh basil, coarsely chopped
Freshly ground black pepper (5 good mill twists)
1½ cups grated Parmesan cheese
⅔ cup chicken consommé (see p. 42)

Wash mushrooms with stems well, and drain. Carefully break off stems without damaging caps. Bring a large pot of water to a boil, and add salt, the juice of half a lemon plus the squeezed lemon rind. Add mushroom caps and cook for 10 minutes. Drain.

Chop mushroom stems, prosciutto, salame and ham rather fine, and mix well with herbs, seasonings and 1 cup cheese, retaining ½ cup for later use.

Heap mushroom caps with stuffing. Pour consommé into baking pan, arrange mushrooms in pan, stuffed side up, and bake for 10 minutes in 350°F. oven. When done, drain off consommé and keep for possible later use. Sprinkle remaining Parmesan over mushrooms and broil for 3 minutes.

Serve hot, 6 mushrooms per person. Serves 6.

ASPARAGI ERBA FREDDI, OLIO E LIMONE
Cold Grass Asparagus with Olive Oil and Lemon

1½ pounds fresh grass asparagus
4 tablespoons olive oil
1 lemon
½ tablespoon freshly chopped Italian parsley
Salt and freshly ground black pepper to taste

Trim asparagus and wash under cold water. Cook in boiling salted water for 2 minutes. Drain, run under cold water. Set aside at room temperature.

In a bowl, mix olive oil with the strained lemon juice, add chopped parsley, salt and pepper. Blend well. Place asparagus in a platter large enough to accommodate all, pour dressing over them a half hour before serving.

Serves 6.

CROSTINI DI ACCIUGHE, MORTADELLA E FONTINA

Hot Anchovy, Mortadella and Fontina Canapés

These are frequently served at parties with cocktails or with a properly chilled white wine. They are called *stuzzica appetito*.

12 thin slices white bread
18 filets of anchovies
6 rather thin slices fontina cheese
6 thin slices mortadella
Fresh black pepper
¾ cup olive oil
4 eggs
¼ cup heavy cream
1 tablespoon water
¼ cup grated Parmesan cheese

Trim edges of bread. On each of 6 slices of bread place 3 filets of anchovies, 1 slice of fontina, and 1 slice of mortadella. Shower each slice with 2 turns of the pepper mill and close the sandwiches. Cut each sandwich into 4 triangles.

Heat olive oil over low heat in a frying pan large enough to accommodate all the little sandwiches. Beat eggs in a bowl with the cream, water and Parmesan cheese until well blended. Dip each sandwich in egg batter. By this time oil should be fairly hot. Test with a drop of batter; if it cooks quickly, the temperature is right. Carefully immerse sandwiches in hot oil and fry them until golden-brown.

Drain each sandwich on absorbent paper for a few seconds. Place on serving platter. Serve immediately.

Serves 6.

SARDE MARINATE "ALL'AGIADDA"
Marinated Sardines Genovese Style

Although this is very much a Mediterranean dish, found in Italy, Greece and Spain as well as South France, the preparation here is, to my knowledge, typically Genovese. *All'agiadda* means, in Genovese dialect, "marinated in garlic." You find this dish on every Ligurian osteria or trattoria menu.

This dish can be used as an appetizer or as a main dish, accompanied by a green or cold vegetable salad.

4 pounds fresh, medium-sized sardines
2 cups olive oil
½ cup red wine vinegar
1 teaspoon chopped garlic
Salt and black pepper
2 tablespoons chopped fresh parsley
5 bay leaves
1 teaspoon rosemary, fresh if possible
1 twig fresh tarragon, or ½ teaspoon dried tarragon
½ teaspoon thyme
½ teaspoon juniper berries (optional)
2 cups flour
2½ cups vegetable oil
1 large onion (or 2 medium-sized onions)
2 cloves garlic, peeled

Wash sardines under cold water and scale them. Chop off heads. With a small sharp knife, make insertion in belly of each sardine and clean out entrails as much as possible. The bones may be left in or taken out. Put fish in refrigerator.

Prepare marinade in a flat baking dish, preferably glass. Pour olive oil in dish and add vinegar, chopped garlic, salt and pepper, parsley, bay leaves, rosemary, tarragon, thyme and juniper berries. Blend well and set aside.

Take sardines from refrigerator, wash again under cold water, and dry. Spread flour on piece of aluminum foil; roll sardines in the flour. Fry sardines in 2 cups of the vegetable oil for 6-8 minutes until fish are crisp and have turned a golden color. Remove from pan and drain on paper towels until cool.

Peel onion and slice very thin. Pour remaining ½ cup vegetable oil into frying pan, add garlic, and sauté onions to a golden yellow. Drain and put in dish to cool.

Mix in with marinade and blend well. Place sardines in the baking dish. Spoon the marinade over them, and set aside for 2 hours. Then, carefully turn sardines and again spoon the marinade over them. Cover with foil and place in refrigerator for 24 hours. Take out of refrigerator 2 hours before serving and leave uncovered to bring to room temperature. Spoon marinade over each serving.

Serves 6-10, with approximately 3 sardines per person.

LUMACHE ALLA GINO
Snails Gino

Gino, a former chef of mine, created the sauce for this dish, but he kept it a secret in spite of any clues I was able to extract from waiters and kitchen help. Bit by bit I reconstructed the recipe and then tricked Gino into tasting it, under the pretext that it was his own and needed the seasoning corrected. "Perfect," he said. I knew that I had it.

3 tablespoons tarragon leaves, fresh or preserved in vinegar
1 tablespoon red wine vinegar
24 tablespoons butter (¾ pound)
1½ teaspoons chopped garlic
1½ tablespoons chopped parsley
Pinch thyme
½ teaspoon dry basil
5 drops Tabasco Sauce
1½ tablespoons Worcestershire Sauce
1½ tablespoons A-1 Sauce
1 cup Brown Sauce (see p. 187)
Salt and pepper
3 cans snails (24 in can)

Simmer tarragon in red wine vinegar until completely dry, almost crisp. Chop finely and set aside. Melt butter in a saucepan, add garlic, and cook to a golden color. Combine parsley and other herbs, including tarragon, and continue cooking over low flame. Add Worcestershire, A-1 and Brown sauces. Cook 20 minutes. Season with salt and pepper.

Drain snails. Wash thoroughly under cold water until completely clean. Pour snails into sauce. Cook over a low flame for 5-6 minutes. Serve very hot, 12 on a plate. They can also be served in individual ramekins.

Serves 6.

CARPACCIO
Pounded Shell Steak

Carpaccio, very thin slices of raw beef (shell steak), is a specialty in Venice, Rome and Milan, not often found in other parts of Italy. Originated at Harry's Bar in Venice, it is served mainly in fine restaurants and hotels rather than in private homes. The sauce is my creation.

3 pounds shell steak in one piece, boned and trimmed of all fat

2 egg yolks
Juice of 1 lemon
¼ teaspoon salt
Pinch white pepper
¾ cup olive oil
1 teaspoon finely chopped fresh tarragon, or ½ teaspoon dried
    tarragon
1 teaspoon chopped fresh parsley
2 drops Tabasco Sauce
1 teaspoon Worcestershire Sauce
½ teaspoon A-1 Sauce
1½ teaspoons ketchup

It is preferable to have the shell steak boned by the butcher, but the rest of the preparation can be done at home. Simply cut off the tail piece of the steak, and with a sharp knife remove every bit of fat. The steak, completely lean, is then ready for slicing. The tail piece can be used for stew at a later time.

When steak is completely trimmed, cut into thin slices. Three pounds should provide 12 to 14 slices. Place each slice between pieces of aluminum foil and pound with a wooden mallet until meat is wafer thin. Arrange slices on plate and refrigerate.

For the mayonnaise sauce, blend egg yolks with the juice of the lemon (carefully strained) and season with salt and pepper. Beat with a wire whisk and slowly stir in olive oil, beginning with a tablespoon at a time. When sauce begins to thicken, add herbs, Tabasco, Worcestershire and A-1 sauces, and ketchup. Continue beating until sauce reaches a very smooth, thick consistency. If possible, prepare sauce in a glass bowl with a round bottom set in a larger bowl filled with ice. This creates a much better texture.

Serve 2 slices of meat per person with mayonnaise sauce on the side. Carpaccio may be offered as an appetizer, or as a main dish served with either fresh cold asparagus or an arugula salad.

Serves 6-7.

FRITTATA DI ZUCCHINI, FONTINA E PROSCIUTTO
Fried Zucchini with Fontina and Prosciutto

3 medium zucchini
2 tablespoons olive oil
4 eggs
¼ cup heavy cream
¼ pound fontina cheese, diced
4 slices prosciutto, cut in julienne strips
Freshly ground black pepper to taste
Pinch salt

Wash zucchini well under cold water, chop off tips, and discard. Slice zucchini in ¼-inch thick rounds. In a frying pan, heat 1 tablespoon oil; fry sliced zucchini until golden, turning them several times. Drain on paper towel, and set aside. Beat eggs;

add cream, fontina, strips of prosciutto, pepper and salt. Fold in zucchini and mix gently. Let stand for about 10 minutes.

Heat ½ tablespoon olive oil in a 6-inch omelet pan and, when hot, add zucchini and egg mixture. Cook approximately 15 minutes over low flame, making sure egg does not stick to pan. Next, place pan under broiler just long enough to set top crust, being careful it does not burn.

Turn frittata upside down into a dish. Wipe pan clean of any egg residue; add remaining ½ tablespoon of oil to pan, and heat. Replace frittata in pan, bottom side up, and cook over low flame another 10 minutes. When done, frittata should be about 1½ inches thick. Place on paper towel to absorb oil.

Serves 6.

ZUCCHINI RIPIENI DEL GENOVESE
Stuffed Zucchini Genovese Style

This is a truly Genovese dish. Stuffed vegetables are typical of Liguria.

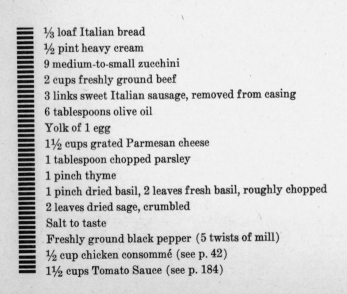

⅓ loaf Italian bread
½ pint heavy cream
9 medium-to-small zucchini
2 cups freshly ground beef
3 links sweet Italian sausage, removed from casing
6 tablespoons olive oil
Yolk of 1 egg
1½ cups grated Parmesan cheese
1 tablespoon chopped parsley
1 pinch thyme
1 pinch dried basil, 2 leaves fresh basil, roughly chopped
2 leaves dried sage, crumbled
Salt to taste
Freshly ground black pepper (5 twists of mill)
½ cup chicken consommé (see p. 42)
1½ cups Tomato Sauce (see p. 184)

Soak bread in cream. Wash zucchini thoroughly, cut off ends and split in half lengthwise. Carefully scoop out pulp, setting aside 2 tablespoons and discarding the rest.

Sauté ground beef and sausage meat, along with the 2 tablespoons of pulp, in 2½ tablespoons of olive oil, leaving the mixture undercooked. Place in a large bowl and combine with bread, egg yolk, 1 cup of cheese (putting aside remaining ½ cup), parsley, herbs and seasonings. Mix by breaking everything up with your fingers and leaving it all rather coarse. Stuff zucchini shells generously and place them, stuffing side up, in a baking pan containing remaining 3½ tablespoons olive oil and all of the consommé.

Bake in 350°F. oven about 20 minutes or until shells are tender and tops of stuffing appear well browned. Drain liquid from pan (liquid can be saved and used as a base for other sauces), and pour tomato sauce evenly over the zucchini. Sprinkle with remaining Parmesan cheese. Place baking pan in broiler for 3 minutes, or until Parmesan cheese is melted and rather brown. Serve 3 pieces of zucchini per person.

Serves 6.

CRUDEZZE CON BAGNA CAUDA
Raw Vegetables with Hot Anchovy Dip

Crudezze con bagna cauda originated in the Piedmont region of Italy. It is strictly a wintertime dish, usually accompanied by homemade salami, sausage and hot bread.

6 raw carrots, scraped
1 medium bunch celery, scraped
3 cucumbers, peeled
1 bunch red radishes
2 heads Belgian endive
1 bunch white radishes
3 peppers (1 red, 1 green, 1 yellow), seeded
8 medium mushrooms
1 bunch watercress
1 large fennel
Package fresh alfalfa

SAUCE

1½ cups olive oil

8 tablespoons butter (¼ pound)

5 filets of anchovies

1 teaspoon chopped garlic

1½ tablespoons chopped parsley

3 leaves fresh basil, or 1 teaspoon dried basil

½ teaspoon chopped fresh tarragon, or 1 pinch dried tarragon

2 tablespoons red wine vinegar

Freshly ground black pepper (6-7 twists of mill)

1 tablespoon medium-sized capers

Wash all vegetables thoroughly; cut carrots, celery, cucumbers and endive into long strips. Take root ends off radishes. Cut peppers into 8 slices lengthwise, and mushrooms into quarters (leaving stems on). Thick stems of watercress should be discarded. Fennel leaves should be cut off, and fennel quartered. Arrange in salad bowl and garnish with alfalfa.

Mix oil and butter in sauté pan. Add anchovy filets and garlic, and cook over low flame until garlic begins to be golden and anchovies soften to a paste. Then stir in herbs and vinegar. Add pepper and capers.

Serve crudezze con bagna cauda as a dip. The bagna cauda should be kept hot in a chafing dish over an alcohol flame or on an electric warming tray.

Serves 6-7.

FINOCCHIONA E PERE
Finocchiona and Pears

Finocchiona is a special Tuscan salame not easily found, but prosciutto or coppa dolce can be substituted.

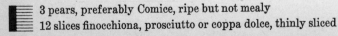

3 pears, preferably Comice, ripe but not mealy

12 slices finocchiona, prosciutto or coppa dolce, thinly sliced

Peel and core pears, cut in quarters. Place them in large platter, cover with slices of finocchiona, prosciutto or coppa dolce.
Serves 6.

CARCIOFI ALLA ROMANA
Artichokes Roman Style

Among the gifts Cleopatra took to Rome were baskets brimming with beautiful artichokes from Judea. The Romans immediately invented a way to cook them. Unfortunately, the artichokes grown in the United States are of a different breed and not as tender as those obtainable in Rome. But they can still make a satisfying dish.

6 medium artichokes
1 lemon, juice and rind
1½ cups olive oil
1 tablespoon chopped fresh garlic
1 cup freshly chopped parsley
2 cups chicken consommé (see p. 42)
Salt to taste
Freshly ground black pepper (6-7 twists)

Neatly chop off artichoke tops, remove tough outer leaves and cut off stems. Add juice of lemon plus rind to a large pot of boiling salted water. Immerse artichokes in water, occasionally pressing them down with a wooden spoon—*do not leave them unattended*—and cook for 10 minutes.

Remove artichokes from water one by one and drain them by placing them upside down in a pan. When drained, place them upright in a baking pan. In separate bowl, mix oil, garlic, parsley, consommé, salt and pepper, and pour mixture over artichokes. Place pan in preheated 400°F oven and cook 15 minutes, or until outer leaves begin to turn a copper color; then place pan under broiler for 3 minutes.

Serve in a soup dish. Pour remaining juice over artichokes.
Serves 6.

PEPERONI STILE BIFFI
Stuffed Peppers Biffi

Il Ristorante Biffi has been located in the Galleria Vittorio Emanuele II in Milan since the latter part of the nineteenth century. Until the 1950s it was a first-class restaurant, and its patrons were the glittering superstars of the nearby La Scala, eminent composers, writers, movie directors, the beautiful soubrettes of the *varietá* houses and the inevitable motley groups of hangers-on.

The menu always featured a most elaborate buffet that included Peperoni Stile Biffi. Unfortunately, Biffi's has now been converted into a sort of self-service restaurant, featuring such fare as pizza, hot dogs and packaged potato chips. The famous peperoni are no longer to be found, but their memory is well worth preserving.

¼ loaf Italian bread, in rough hunks

1 pint heavy cream

6 medium-to-large sweet red peppers (or green, if red are not available)

8 filets of anchovies

3 pieces canned whole red pimiento

¼ cup medium-sized capers

⅓ cup chopped parsley

3 3½-ounce cans Genova tuna, flaked, undrained*

½ cup pitted black olives, roughly chopped

Pinch oregano

Pinch nutmeg

Pepper to taste

1 cup grated Parmesan cheese

¼ cup olive oil

1 cup beef or chicken consommé (see p. 42)

Soak bread in cream. Cut off tops of peppers and clean insides of all seeds and fibers; shave bottoms slightly so that peppers

---

* Drain if using American tuna.

will stand up in baking pan. Wash peppers well under running cold water. Dry.

Prepare stuffing: coarsely grind anchovies, pimiento, capers and soaked bread. Place mixture in mixing bowl and add parsley, tuna, olives, oregano, nutmeg, pepper and all but 4 tablespoons of the cheese. Mix thoroughly, then stuff peppers with mixture.

Put olive oil and consommé in a deep baking pan. Carefully stand peppers in pan and cover with aluminum foil. Bake 15 minutes in 400°F oven; then uncover and bake about 5 to 8 minutes until a firm crust is formed on the tops.

Before serving, sprinkle remaining grated cheese over tops and place under broiler for 2 minutes. Serve hot.

Serves 6.

FRITTATA DI SPINACI E PROSCIUTTO
Spinach and Prosciutto Frittata

In Italy, on the day after Easter Sunday, called "Pasquetta," people generally take to the hills and gather for grand picnics on the new grass, a pagan rite of spring that goes back to the Romans. A frittata is one of the featured dishes in everyone's picnic basket. Frittata of spinach is a great favorite.

3 eggs
¼ cup heavy cream
½ cup grated Parmesan cheese
3 slices prosciutto cut in julienne strips
Freshly ground black pepper to taste
¼ pound fresh, carefully washed raw spinach, or ¼ package
    defrosted frozen spinach
2 tablespoons olive oil

Beat eggs, and add cream, cheese, strips of prosciutto and pepper. Fold in spinach (if raw, chop roughly), and mix well. Let stand for about 10 minutes. Heat 1 tablespoon olive oil in a 6-inch omelet pan and, when hot, add egg mixture. Cook approximately 15 minutes over low flame, making sure egg does not stick to pan. Next, place pan under broiler just long enough to set top crust, being careful it does not burn.

Turn frittata upside down into a dish. Wipe sauté pan clean of any egg residue, add the second tablespoon of oil to the pan and heat. Replace frittata in pan, bottom side up, and cook over low heat another 10-15 minutes. When done, frittata should be about 1 inch thick. Dry on absorbent paper towel so that it will not be oily.

Serve hot with a good mixed green salad in an oil and vinegar dressing, as an appetizer, luncheon dish or snack. Frittata can also be served at room temperature.

Serves 4 as an appetizer, or 1 as a main dish.

INSALATA DI RISO
Rice Salad

½ tablespoon pignoli
2 cups Arborio rice
1 7-ounce can tuna packed in oil (preferably Genova or Pastene), undrained*
¼ pound boiled ham, cubed
½ cup Gaeta olives, pitted
½ cup grated Parmesan cheese
½ tablespoon chopped parsley
2 pieces pimiento, chopped coarsely
Pinch nutmeg
⅓ cup olive oil
Salt and pepper

Sauté pignoli with a few drops of olive oil until lightly browned. Cook rice approximately 25 minutes or until *al dente*. Break up tuna with a fork, then combine with all the ingredients in a salad bowl, and mix well. Serve at room temperature.

Serves 6.

---

* Drain if using American tuna.

FAGIOLI E TONNO
Beans and Tuna

2 pounds fresh cranberry beans, shelled and washed; or 3 cups
   of dried cranberry beans, presoaked in cold water; or
   2 17-ounce cans cannellini, drained
2 7-ounce cans tuna packed in oil (preferably Genova or Pastene),
   undrained*
⅓ cup olive oil
1 tablespoon red wine vinegar
⅓ teaspoon chopped garlic
½ small onion, thinly sliced (preferably red Italian onion)
½ tablespoon chopped parsley
Pinch nutmeg
Salt and pepper

Place beans in cold, salted water; bring to a boil, and cook for
20 minutes or until *al dente*. (If using canned beans, simply
drain but do not cook.) Drain cooked beans carefully and cool
at room temperature. In a salad bowl, combine beans with tuna.
Then, add all other ingredients and toss well.
    Serves 6.

GAMBERETTI, LUMACHE E CÈPES IN UMIDO
Baby Shrimp, Snails and French Wild Mushrooms

This is a rather expensive dish because of its ingredients:
shrimp, snails and, above all, the cèpes which are wild mushrooms imported from France, and which here cost an extravagant nine dollars and up per 8-ounce can.

---

* Drain if using American tuna.

1½ pounds small shrimp
10 tablespoons butter
2 shallots, peeled and minced
1 teaspoon chopped fresh tarragon leaves
½ teaspoon freshly chopped coriander
Pinch nutmeg
Pinch ginger
Pinch cayenne pepper
Generous pinch saffron (powdered)
Salt and freshly ground black pepper to taste
½ tablespoon Dijon mustard
¾ cup dry white wine
½ tablespoon chopped fresh Italian parsley
½ cup Brown Sauce (see p. 187)
½ pint heavy cream
3 tablespoons cognac
1 can snails (2 dozen), drained and washed well under cold
    water; dried
2 8-ounce cans cèpes (Wyco Brand), drained of juice; cut the
    large pieces in halves or quarters

Shell and devein shrimp, wash well under cold water, cook for
2 minutes in boiling salted water. Drain, run cold water over,
set aside. In a large saucepan, melt butter, add shallots, cook
until golden. Add tarragon, coriander, and all other spices.
Cook 5 minutes. Add Dijon mustard, blend well, add white wine.
Let wine reduce for 6 minutes. Add parsley, cook 5 minutes.
Add brown sauce, cook 5 minutes. Strain mixture through fine
wire strainer. Add heavy cream, set over low flame and cook
2 minutes, blend well. Add shrimp, snails and cèpes to sauce,
cook 8 minutes. Add cognac and cook 1-2 minutes. Serve very
hot.

    Serves 6.

Brodo—Zuppe

BRODO DI POLLO
Chicken Consommé

- 1 3-pound chicken, washed
- 1 large ripe tomato
- 3 carrots, scraped and washed
- 1 large onion, peeled and cut in half
- 4 stalks celery, washed
- Shells of 2 eggs (to clarify consommé)
- Small bunch parsley, washed
- Salt and pepper

Pour 1½ gallons of cold water into a large pot. Add all the ingredients. Cook for 1 hour or until vegetables are very well done and chicken meat is almost falling off the bones. Skim fat off frequently as it rises to the surface. Pour the liquid through a fine wire strainer. It should be a clear, light golden color. Discard vegetables and egg shells; store chicken for future use (it can be used for stuffing). Store consommé in refrigerator in a screw-top glass container. It will keep for over a week.

Yield: 1 gallon.

BRODO DI CARNE
Beef Consommé

- 2 pounds beef bones, in small pieces
- 1½ pounds beef chuck*
- 1 large ripe tomato
- 3 carrots, scraped and washed
- 1 large onion, peeled and cut in half
- 4 stalks celery, washed
- 2 egg shells (to clarify consommé)
- Small bunch parsley, washed
- Salt and pepper

---

* Beef and chicken can be cooked together to make a rich consommé. The beef should be started ½ hour before the chicken. The meats can be used later as a stuffing for cannelloni.

Pour 1½ gallons of cold water into a large pot. Add beef bones, beef, vegetables, egg shells, parsley, salt and pepper. Cook for 1½ hours. Skim off fat frequently as it rises to the surface. Pour consommé through fine wire strainer. Discard vegetables, egg shells and bones, but store beef for future use. Store consommé in refrigerator in a screw-top glass container. It will keep for over a week.

Yield: 1 gallon.

MINESTRONE ALLA GENOVESE
Minestrone Genovese Style

This is, along with pesto, one of the most typical Ligurian dishes. Minestrone means the "big soup" because of the numerous ingredients used in its preparation. Other vegetables in season may be substituted for those called for here. After the minestrone has cooled to room temperature, it can be stored in the refrigerator for three or four days and reheated.

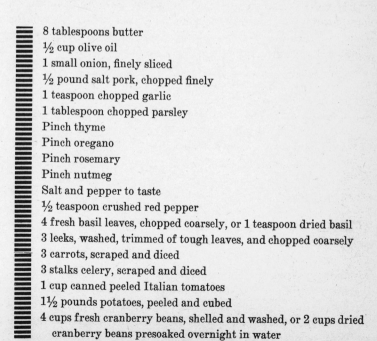

8 tablespoons butter
½ cup olive oil
1 small onion, finely sliced
½ pound salt pork, chopped finely
1 teaspoon chopped garlic
1 tablespoon chopped parsley
Pinch thyme
Pinch oregano
Pinch rosemary
Pinch nutmeg
Salt and pepper to taste
½ teaspoon crushed red pepper
4 fresh basil leaves, chopped coarsely, or 1 teaspoon dried basil
3 leeks, washed, trimmed of tough leaves, and chopped coarsely
3 carrots, scraped and diced
3 stalks celery, scraped and diced
1 cup canned peeled Italian tomatoes
1½ pounds potatoes, peeled and cubed
4 cups fresh cranberry beans, shelled and washed, or 2 cups dried
    cranberry beans presoaked overnight in water

½ small green cabbage, chopped coarsely
½ pound string beans, trimmed and washed
5 medium zucchini, washed and cut in cubes
1 cup fresh peas, shelled
1½ tablespoons Pesto Sauce (see p. 190) (optional)
½ pound short pasta or broken-up spaghetti, or 2 cups Arborio
   rice
½ cup grated Parmesan cheese

Heat butter and oil in a large soup pot over medium flame.
Cook onion until translucent. Add salt pork and cook 10 minutes. Mix in garlic, all herbs and seasonings; make sure they
do not burn. Add leeks, carrots and celery and cook 6 minutes.
Add peeled tomatoes and cook 5 minutes. Add 2½ quarts boiling water. Add potatoes, beans and cabbage and cook 15 minutes. Add string beans, zucchini and peas and cook 10 minutes.
If using pesto, add at this point and simmer another 10 minutes. Set aside.

Cook pasta in 2 quarts salted boiling water until *al dente*. If
using rice, steam until *al dente*. Place some pasta or rice in
each dish and pour well-mixed soup over. Serve with cheese
and freshly ground black pepper.

Serves 10-12.

ZUPPA DI PASTA E FAGIOLI
Pasta and Bean Soup

As many recipes exist for preparing this delectable soup as
there are Italian cities, towns and little villages. It is essentially
a peasant dish and the variations on it are dependent chiefly
on the riches of one's larder. In the summer it is the Florentine
and Roman custom to serve this soup at room temperature.

4 pounds fresh cranberry beans, shelled and washed; or 2 pounds
   dried cranberry beans, soaked overnight in salted water; or
   4 16-ounce cans cannellini
½ small onion, finely sliced
⅔ cup olive oil
¼ teaspoon chopped garlic
¼ teaspoon oregano
½ teaspoon dried basil, or 2 fresh leaves, chopped
Pinch thyme
½ tablespoon chopped parsley
Black pepper
½ teaspoon crushed red pepper
¼ pound pancetta (Italian bacon), cut into chunks
1 stalk celery, washed and finely chopped
1 cup canned peeled Italian tomatoes
6 cups beef consommé (see p. 42)
¾ pound ditalini or tubettini pasta, or any short pasta (even
   broken-up spaghetti)
½ cup grated pecorino (Romano) cheese

If using fresh beans, place them in 2 quarts cold salted water
over medium flame and cook 15-20 minutes until *al dente*. Drain
off all water and set aside. If using dried beans, soak them overnight in salted water. Drain. Place in cold water over medium
flame, and cook approximately 25-30 minutes until *al dente*. If
canned, drain beans of all liquid and set aside.

Cook onion in oil in large soup pot until translucent. Add
garlic and all herbs and seasonings, being careful that they
don't burn. Stir in the pancetta and chopped celery, and cook
until pancetta begins to brown. Add tomatoes and cook for 20
minutes. Then add consommé and bring entire mixture to a boil.

Mix in beans, and bring to a boil again. Then add pasta and
cook until *al dente*. The soup should be rather thick. Serve
with cheese and freshly ground black pepper. Also offer crushed
red pepper. Some people like to pour a teaspoon of olive oil
over each serving.

Serves 6.

ZUPPA DI COZZE
Mussel Soup

½ cup olive oil
½ small onion, finely sliced
½ teaspoon chopped garlic
4 tablespoons dry white wine
Salt
½ pound fish heads and bones
½ tablespoon chopped parsley
Pinch oregano
Pinch thyme
Pinch nutmeg
4 or 5 leaves fresh tarragon or ½ teaspoon dried tarragon
¼ teaspoon pepper
4 pounds mussels, thoroughly cleaned in cold water
4 tablespoons butter
1 envelope saffron
1 lemon, cut in 6 sections
Croutons (optional)

Heat oil in a large soup pot and cook onion until translucent. Add garlic and cook until golden. Add wine and let it cook until it evaporates. Add 6 cups water, 1½ teaspoons salt and bring to a boil. Put in fish heads and bones. Place all herbs in small cheesecloth bag together with nutmeg and pepper, and immerse bag in water, with one end tied to the handle of the pot. Cook 25 minutes.

Meanwhile, place mussels in a pot large enough to accommodate them comfortably. Add 2 cups of water, and steam until mussels open. Allow to cool, then scoop out carefully. Place in dish, and set aside.

Strain fish stock through a fine wire strainer, lined with 2 layers of cheesecloth to make certain that no bones go through. Discard bag of herbs. Put clear broth back on flame and add the butter. Let butter melt as the broth comes to a boil. Add mussels and saffron. Cook 5 minutes.

Serve hot with lemon sections. You can also serve it with croutons.

Serves 6.

TORTELLINI IN BRODO
Tortellini in Broth

Tortellini in brodo is a soup served on holidays in Italian homes, but it is found daily on restaurant menus.

2 quarts chicken consommé (see p. 42)
2 packages tortellini (about 100 pieces), or homemade tortellini
   (see p. 70)
⅓ cup grated Parmesan cheese
Freshly ground black pepper

Bring consommé to a boil. Add tortellini and cook 5-6 minutes. If tortellini are homemade, cook for no more than 2 minutes.
   Divide tortellini equally in individual bowls (approximately 17 per portion), and pour in broth. Serve with cheese and freshly ground pepper.
   Serves 6.

STRACCIATELLA ALLA ROMANA
Roman Egg and Spinach Soup

3 eggs
½ cup grated Parmesan cheese
Salt and pepper
2 quarts beef or chicken consommé (see p. 42)
1½ pounds fresh, carefully washed leaf spinach (with tough
   stems discarded) or 1 package frozen leaf spinach, defrosted

Beat together the eggs and 1 tablespoon Parmesan cheese, and season with salt and pepper. Bring consommé to a boil. Add spinach and return to a boil. Fold in the egg mixture, making sure to blend well. As soon as eggs are cooked (1½ minutes), remove from heat. Serve with remaining cheese and freshly ground pepper.
   Serves 6.

Pasta and Pasta Dishes

PASTA

The making of pasta is regarded as an art among Italian chefs. They often have contests to see who can make the thinnest sheet of pasta, the widest variety of shapes, the most subtle differences in taste. Many kinds of vegetables are used in making special pastas, either dried or fresh, such as artichokes, spinach, tomatoes, beets, zucchini and potatoes. Such ingredients create further variations in taste and texture. And, of course, a good pasta often becomes a great pasta when it is complemented by a delicious and inventive sauce.

Pasta Buying and Storing

DRIED OR PACKAGED PASTA: I recommend buying only imported Italian brands whenever possible. My favorite brands are Di-Cecco, Agnesi and Cirio. These pastas retain their texture and freshness longer than domestic pastas; they are generally of a slightly darker color. Of the American packaged pastas, I would recommend LaRosa and Buitoni.

Packaged pasta should be stored in a cool, dry spot in the kitchen and never refrigerated.

FRESH PASTA: My supplier of pasta, fresh or packaged, is Raffetto, a family-owned, almost one-hundred-year-old store located at 144 West Houston Street in Greenwich Village, New York City. The fresh varieties of pasta—fettuccine, fettuccelle, tagliarini, tortellini, pansoti, and ravioli—are made to my specifications. (I do not make fresh pasta in any of my restaurants for the simple reason that my kitchens lack space. Those of you familiar with my restaurants will understand this!) By all means try to track down a supplier, or learn to make pasta yourself (see below). Fresh pasta should be refrigerated and not kept for more than two days.

FROZEN PASTA: I am opposed to using frozen pasta. Once defrosted, it loses a great deal of texture and flavor.

BASIC RECIPE FOR FRESH PASTA

There are several ways in which pasta can be made, and the method you choose depends on your kitchen equipment, your work space, and your taste. There are those who feel that nothing can equal the quality of pasta kneaded, rolled and cut entirely by hand, as it has been done in Italian households for generations. But it requires technique, which can of course be mastered with practice, and it demands a good-sized work area of at least 18 x 30 inches. However, you can produce a satisfactory pasta in other ways: You can prepare the dough by hand, in a food processor or in an electric mixer equipped with a dough hook; and you can roll it out and cut it by hand, in a manual pasta machine or in an electric pasta machine.

As I've said, I use none of these methods in my restaurants, but the pasta I buy at Raffetto's is excellent and it's made fresh daily. If you have such a source in your neighborhood, use it. But for those of you who must depend on your own labor, here are the various ways to make fresh pasta.

INGREDIENTS:

    4 cups all-purpose flour, preferably unbleached
    4 extra-large eggs
    4 tablespoons olive oil
    Pinch of salt

To make by hand: Form a mound of the flour on a pastry board or worktable, and make a well in the center. Break the eggs into it, and add the olive oil and salt. Break up the eggs with a fork, and with the other hand start to mix in the flour from the top, adding it steadily so that the mixture does not stick to the work surface. When the flour is almost totally absorbed, begin kneading, pressing with the heels of your palms and folding the dough until it is well blended and smooth but still moist. Let pasta dry for 10 minutes. Divide into 4 pieces.

NOTE: What you have just made is the dough for what is known as "yellow pasta." If you should wish to make green or red dough, follow these directions:

PASTA VERDE (GREEN PASTA): Use the ingredients for yellow pasta in the same proportions, but add 8 ounces of fresh spinach.

Remove stems from spinach. Wash leaves thoroughly in cold water, and drain. Bring 1 gallon of salted water to boil, add spinach leaves and cook for 8 minutes. Drain, cool under cold

Tre Garibaldini
redone with Art
Nouveau wallpaper
risotto Mantovana
(with sausage mmm.)
Scotch √ Steak Tartar
Salmon mixed salad
         much improved
         since our last
              visit

running water, and squeeze dry. Chop spinach very fine, measure 1 heaping tablespoon, and place it in the well formed with the flour. Add the eggs, oil and salt, and follow the procedure described on page 51. Let pasta verde dry 5 minutes longer than the yellow pasta.

PASTA ROSSA (RED PASTA): Use the ingredients on page 51 for yellow pasta in the same proportions, but add 1 medium-sized red beet.

Trim the stem of the beet, leaving 1½–2 inches, and wash beet very well under cold water. Bring ½ gallon of salted water to boil, add the beet, and cook about 1 hour or until tender. Skin under cold water, discard stem, then chop beet very fine. Measure 1 heaping tablespoon, and place in the well formed with the flour, add the eggs, oil and salt, and follow the procedure described on page 51. Let pasta rossa dry 5-8 minutes longer than yellow pasta.

To roll out the pasta: The best rolling pin to use for this is about 30 inches long and 6 inches round; but you can also use a long, tapered pastry rolling pin; or the longest available rotating rolling pin.

Dust the pastry board with some sifted flour. Roll out each ball of dough to a uniform thickness of ⅟₁₆ to ⅟₃₂ of an inch— or as thin as you can get it—in the following way: First roll it into a flattened oval. Then turn and roll the dough several times until it is completely round. Dust it with flour and turn it over. Again roll out and turn, dust with flour, and turn over. Repeat this procedure about 5 times. After the second or third rolling out, it will be difficult to lift and turn the pasta by hand. Therefore gently wrap it around the rolling pin and unroll it on the reverse side. When the dough is thin enough, roll out the edges to give uniform thickness.

Allow to dry on the pastry board for 12-15 minutes before cutting, unless you are making tortellini.

To make in an electric mixer with a dough hook: Put all ingredients in the mixer bowl, and attach the dough hook. Mix at low speed for 3-4 minutes. Then scrape down any loose dough, and knead for another minute. Form into a ball, and knead by hand for a few seconds to achieve a smooth, well-blended dough. Divide into 4 pieces. Roll out as directed above or in a pasta machine.

To make in an electric food processor: Follow the manufac-
turer's instructions for making egg noodles, dividing the recipe
into at least 2 batches, according to the amount of flour your
processor can accommodate. Put all ingredients in the mixing
container, and blend them for 15 seconds. Stop the machine
and press some of the dough between thumb and finger to see
if it will adhere. It may need a little more flour if it is too
sticky or a touch more egg if it does not hold together. Form
into a ball and knead by hand on a lightly floured board or
between the rollers of a pasta machine. Roll out and allow to
dry 12-15 minutes before cutting.

To use a pasta machine: Both the manual and electric pasta
machines operate on the same principle. There are two rollers
for kneading and rolling out the dough and either two or three
cutters for making pasta of various widths.

After the pasta has been mixed by any of the methods described above, divide it into 4 smooth pieces. Set the rollers at
the widest opening, and run each piece through at least 8 times,
folding in half after each pass, to knead the dough. Divide into
8 pieces. Then make the space between the rollers one notch
smaller, and run the dough through again. Continue this process, adjusting the setting another notch smaller each time, until
the pasta has achieved the thickness you want. (My preference
is the thickness of 3 sheets of writing paper.) As you roll out
the sheets place them on a dishtowel or waxed paper, and let
them rest for 10-15 minutes—unless you are making tortellini,
where the dough must be as flexible as possible—and then proceed to cut.

TO CUT PASTA:

CANNELLONI AND MANICOTTI—cut into 4 x 4-inch squares.

LASAGNE—cut into strips 4 x 20 inches.

FETTUCCINE—if cutting by hand, fold up each piece of pasta
gently into a flattened roll, and cut into ¼-inch strips. Unfold
and place on a dishtowel to dry. Or run through the ¼-inch
cutting section of a pasta machine.

FETTUCCELLE—cut by hand as for fettuccine in a slightly narrower width or run through the appropriate cutting section of a
pasta machine, if you have one that is equipped with 3 cutters.

TAGLIARINI—cut by hand as for fettuccine into ⅟₁₆-inch strips,
or run through the ⅟₁₆-inch cutter of a pasta machine.

TORTELLINI—in this case, do not let the pasta dry. Cut immediately into circles, 1½ inches in diameter, with a round cookie cutter. Proceed to fill as directed on page 70.

RAVIOLI AND PANSOTI—lay the pasta on a pastry board or table. With a jagged-edged cutting wheel, cut lengthwise into strips 3 inches wide. Proceed to fill as directed on pages 67 & 76.

AGNOLOTTI—lay the past on o pastry board or table. With a jagged-edged cutting wheel, cut lengthwise into strips 3 inches wide. Proceed to fill as directed on page 57.

PASTA DISHES

RIPIENO PER AGNOLOTTI
Agnolotti Filling

½ cup olive oil
1 clove garlic, peeled
½ pound lean beef, such as eye of round
1 chicken breast, boned and skinned
10 tablespoons butter
⅓ teaspoon nutmeg
½ tablespoon chopped parsley
Salt and pepper to taste
½ cup red wine
½ pound prosciutto, sliced
2 eggs
½ cup Parmesan
Fresh pasta (see pgs. 50–56)

Heat oil in a skillet, add garlic; brown the beef thoroughly, remove and set aside. Then brown the chicken breast; remove and set aside. Discard garlic. Melt the butter in the skillet; then return the beef and chicken. Add nutmeg, parsley, salt and pepper. Cook for 10 minutes. Add wine and let it evaporate. Add prosciutto and cook 3 minutes. Let cool. Then put through the coarse setting of a meat grinder. Fold in the eggs and Parmesan cheese. Blend well.

Prepare fresh pasta and cut as directed for agnolotti.

To assemble: lay strips of pasta on a pastry board or table. Place 1 teaspoon mounds of filling at 1½-inch intervals down the center of each strip. Moisten the edges of the dough and the spaces between the filling with water. Carefully fold the strips in half to cover the filling. Press along the moistened dough to seal the mounds thoroughly. Then cut into half-moons —do not cut the folded edge—using an inverted glass or a cookie cutter. Press cut edges to seal. Allow agnolotti to dry for at least 20 minutes before cooking. Dust with sifted flour.

AGNOLOTTI AL RAGÙ E FUNGHI
Agnolotti with Ragù and Mushrooms

This richly filled pasta, shaped like a half-moon, is typical of the region of Emilia, which is also the source of Italy's best dried mushrooms.

2½ cups Ragù (see p. 184)
½ cup dry mushrooms, presoaked (see p. 13)
½ tablespoon chopped parsley
Fresh agnolotti (see fresh pasta, pgs. 50–56 and Agnolotti
    Filling p. 57), or packaged agnolotti (5 packages of 50
    agnolotti each)
1 tablespoon butter
⅓ cup Parmesan cheese
Freshly ground black pepper

Pour ragù into a saucepan and heat over low flame for 5 minutes; add mushrooms and parsley, cook 10 minutes, set aside and keep warm. Bring 1 gallon of salted water to boil. Cook fresh agnolotti 2½ minutes; if using dry agnolotti, cook 8-10 minutes. Drain. Melt butter in frying pan. Add 5 tablespoons of the ragù, and mix well with agnolotti. Pour remaining sauce over pasta in serving platter.

Serves 6-8.

CANNELLONI DEL BOLOGNESE
Stuffed Pasta Alla Bolognese

This recipe came to me via L'Osteria del Cavallino in Savona. The Bolognese origin is dubious, since the chef of that establishment was a large lady from Piedmont. In any case, I was one of the first to introduce this delicious dish to New York, at a time when northern Italian cooking was little known in restaurants around the city.

1 small chicken, about 2 pounds
1 pound fresh leaf spinach, or ½ package frozen leaf spinach,
    chopped coarsely

BOLOGNESE SAUCE:
1 carrot, scraped and washed
1 stalk celery, scraped and washed
½ small onion
¼ cup olive oil
5 tablespoons butter
¼ teaspoon chopped garlic
3 leaves fresh basil or ½ teaspoon dried basil
Pinch rosemary
1 tablespoon chopped parsley
1 bay leaf
Pinch thyme
Pinch nutmeg
½ teaspoon salt
¼ teaspoon pepper
¾ pound chuck beef, in 1 piece
¾ pound shoulder pork, in 1 piece
⅓ cup beef consommé (see p. 42)
¼ cup red wine
3½ cups Tomato Sauce (see p. 184)
10 slices mozzarella cheese, ⅛ inch thick
1 egg
6 pieces Italian dried mushrooms, presoaked (see p. 13), chopped
    coarsely
2 cups Parmesan cheese

Fresh pasta (see pgs. 50–55)
1 tablespoon vegetable oil
2½ cups Cream Sauce (see p. 191)

Place chicken in 3 quarts cold salted water and bring to boil.
Then lower heat and simmer for about ½ hour until tender.

If fresh spinach is used, remove stems, wash leaves thoroughly. Cook 3-5 minutes in 2 cups salted boiling water. If
frozen is used, simply let defrost at room temperature. In
either case, squeeze free of water and chop coarsely.

For Bolognese sauce: put carrot, celery stalk and onion through grinder or food processor. Heat olive oil and butter over low flame in large saucepan. Combine chopped garlic, basil, rosemary, parsley, bay leaf, thyme, nutmeg, salt and pepper, onion, carrot and celery mixture, and cook for 20 minutes. Then place beef and pork in the pan (still over low flame) and cook for 20 minutes, adding a few spoonfuls of consommé and the red wine while cooking. Make sure meat does not stick to pan. After wine has evaporated (you will no longer smell it), and meat is tender, add tomato sauce. Cook another 20 minutes. Remove bay leaf and discard. Remove meat from sauce. Strain sauce carefully through a food mill. Then, on a very low flame, simmer for another 10 minutes.

Chop meat rather coarsely. Remove skin from chicken and detach the breast meat.* Also chop coarsely. Reserve remaining chicken and chicken stock for other uses. Chop 2 slices of mozzarella. Put meat, chicken and mozzarella in mixing bowl; add egg, mushrooms, spinach and ¾ cup Parmesan cheese. Blend thoroughly, preferably with your hands. Set mixture aside.

Prepare pasta and cut according to directions for cannelloni. You should have 16–18 squares.

Bring to boil a gallon of salted water; add 1 tablespoon vegetable oil. Carefully immerse the pasta squares, one at a time, and cook 2 minutes. Gently drain and run under cold water. Place squares on work counter. Place 1½ tablespoons of filling in the center of each pasta square and form into a roll.

Preheat oven to 350°F.

In a baking pan, pour a layer of Bolognese sauce; place cannelloni side by side, then cover with another layer of sauce. (Any remaining sauce can be saved for later use.) Spoon Béchamel sauce over the cannelloni. Cut the remaining 8 slices of mozzarella into strips; each strip should cover 1 cannelloni. Cook cannelloni in preheated oven for 10 minutes.

Serve very hot, 2 pieces of cannelloni per person, making sure to spoon the sauce around each portion. Serve with remaining cheese and fresh pepper.

Serves 8.

---

* You may use 2 small, boned chicken breasts instead of a whole chicken, in which case poach the breasts in 2 tablespoons butter to prevent drying. Do not overcook.

CANNELLONI DI MARE
Cannelloni with Seafood Filling

FILLING:
2 tablespoons butter
½ pound cooked crabmeat, broken up with fork
½ pound small cooked shrimp, peeled, deveined and chopped
    coarsely
Cooked meat of 1 lobster tail, or meat from small can of lobster,
    chopped coarsely
3 pieces dried mushrooms, presoaked (see p. 13)
4 fresh mushrooms, washed and chopped coarsely
1 tablespoon chopped parsley
2 leaves fresh basil, chopped; or pinch dried basil
Pinch nutmeg
Pinch ginger
Salt and pepper
1 egg yolk
1 tablespoon vegetable oil

Fresh pasta (see pgs. 50–55)
¾ cup Tomato Sauce (see p. 184)
2½ cups Cream Sauce (see p. 191)
1 cup grated Parmesan cheese

Melt butter in a frying pan, add crabmeat, shrimp, lobster, dried and fresh mushrooms, herbs, spices, salt and pepper. Sauté for 5 minutes, mixing well. Set aside to cool. Mix in egg yolk and ¾ cup Parmesan cheese.

Prepare fresh pasta and cut according to directions for cannelloni. You will need 12–16 squares. (I usually make green pasta for this dish.)

Add oil to a large pot of salted, boiling water and drop in, one at a time, each square of pasta. Cook 2 minutes. Drain gently, run under cold water, making sure squares don't break or stick together. Spread pasta squares on work counter, place 1½ tablespoons of the seafood stuffing in the center of each square, and form into a roll. Pour tomato sauce into a baking dish; arrange the cannelloni in the sauce and cover with cream sauce. Sprinkle with remaining Parmesan cheese. Bake in oven preheated to 350°F. for 8 minutes. Serve 2 cannelloni per person; spoon sauce over each portion.

Serves 6-8.

FETTUCCINE ALL'ALFREDO

Not my own dish, but named after the founder of Alfredo's in Rome. The dish is also called Fettuccine Alla Panna (with heavy cream).

1½ pounds fresh green or white fettuccine (see pgs. 50–55), or imported dried fettuccine
6 tablespoons butter
½ pint heavy cream
3 egg yolks
¾ cup grated Parmesan cheese
Freshly ground pepper

Cook fettuccine in 1 gallon salted boiling water for 1½ minutes if fresh, 5-6 minutes if dried. Drain well. Melt butter in large frying pan over medium flame. Toss fettuccine in pan to coat heavily with butter. Cook 1 minute, stir in cream and cook for another 1 minute. Add egg yolks and mix quickly to avoid scrambling eggs. Add ½ cup Parmesan cheese and mix well. Serve with remaining Parmesan cheese and freshly ground pepper.

Serves 6-8.

FETTUCCELLE (or SPAGHETTINI) ALLA PUTTANESCA

The adjective *puttanesca* has various meanings in Italian: in the manner of a whore, seductive or lascivious, like the arts of a *puttana*; or a mixture of various ingredients and flavors.

Puttanesca, therefore, is an improvised sauce full of surprises that bears no relation to any classical sauce. I believe its origins are in the South Italian kitchen.

3 tablespoons olive oil
8 tablespoons butter
1 teaspoon chopped garlic
8 anchovy filets, minced
1½ cups imported Italian peeled tomatoes, drained
Freshly ground black pepper
¼ cup capers, drained
¾ cup pitted Gaeta olives
2 7-ounce cans Italian tuna in olive oil, undrained*
1 tablespoon chopped parsley
Pinch oregano
2 fresh basil leaves, chopped; or generous pinch dried basil
Approximately 1½ pounds homemade fettuccelle (see pgs. 50–55), dried fettuccelle, or spaghettini
½ cup grated Parmesan cheese

Heat oil and 4 tablespoons of butter in a saucepan. Add garlic and cook quickly without browning. Add minced anchovies and cook 3 minutes. Then add tomatoes and pepper to taste, and cook 15 minutes. Stir in capers, olives and broken-up tuna until well blended. Add parsley, oregano and basil. Cook 5 minutes. Add remaining butter and cook 10 minutes longer. Set aside and keep warm.

Bring 1 gallon of salted water to boil, cook homemade fettuccelle 1½ minutes; cook dried fettuccelle 5 minutes. If using spaghettini, cook 6 minutes. Drain well.

Spoon a little of the sauce into a frying pan over low heat, add pasta and toss well. Lay on a serving dish; pour the remaining sauce over. Serve with Parmesan cheese and freshly ground pepper.

Serves 6-8.

---

* Drain if using American tuna.

LASAGNE DI CARNEVALE
Stuffed Lasagne

Stuffed lasagne for the Mardi Gras! It's a meal for parties, to be consumed with robust red wines. It's a meal of *allegria*. A waltz afterward, therefore, is in order.

SAUCE:

1 cup Italian dry mushrooms, presoaked (see p. 13)
8 tablespoons butter
⅓ cup olive oil
1 clove garlic, peeled
1 pound pork sausage, removed from casing and crumbled
½ pound loin of pork, finely ground
1 pound ground beef
1 tablespoon fresh chopped parsley
3–4 fresh basil leaves, finely chopped; or 1½ teaspoons dried
    basil
Pinch thyme
Pinch oregano
Pinch nutmeg
Salt and pepper
½ cup dry red wine
2½ tablespoons tomato paste
2½ cups Tomato Sauce (see p. 184)

1 egg yolk
1 pound ricotta cheese
Fresh pasta (see pgs. 50–55)
1 cup grated Parmesan cheese
1 cup grated pecorino cheese
¼ pound mozzarella cheese, diced small or shredded
¼ pound fonduta cheese, diced small or shredded

Heat all but 1 tablespoon each of butter and olive oil in a deep saucepan. Add garlic and sauté it until browned, then discard; add sausage meat to oil. When sausage begins to brown, add pork and sauté until it, too, is browned. Then add beef and continue to cook for another 15 minutes. Add herbs, spices, salt and pepper, and presoaked mushrooms (squeezed of all water), and cook another 10 minutes, stirring with a wooden spoon. Add wine, and cook until it is evaporated.

Dilute tomato paste with ½ cup warm water and stir into sauce. Cook 15 minutes; then add tomato sauce, cook 20 minutes. Salt and pepper to taste.

Beat egg yolk into ricotta until smooth. Have other cheeses properly prepared and ready for use.

Prepare fresh pasta and cut according to directions for lasagne. Bring large pot of salted water to boil and add the remaining tablespoon of oil to the water so that the pasta will not stick together. Drop sheets of pasta, *a sheet at a time*, into the water and cook 2 minutes. Drain carefully, then rinse under cold water, separating the pieces from each other. Set aside.

Brush a deep fireproof baking dish (large enough to accommodate the lasagne) with remaining tablespoon of butter. Ladle some of sauce into dish to cover bottom. Place sheets of pasta on bottom of dish in such a way that they cover the bottom and also drape over sides of dish. Spread sauce over pasta. Sprinkle a layer each of Parmesan, pecorino, mozzarella, fonduta, and finally ricotta, and cover with another layer of pasta (this time omitting the draping). Being careful to reserve ½ cup of sauce, repeat layering procedure until rest of sauce, cheese and pasta are used up and dish is filled. Then fold draped pasta over top and smooth on remaining sauce. Bake in preheated 350°F oven for 10 minutes. Serve with additional grated Parmesan, if you like.

Serves 8-10.

RIPIENO PER MANICOTTI
Manicotti Filling

1 pound whole-milk ricotta
2 cups grated Parmesan cheese
¼ pound prosciutto, chopped coarsely
½ tablespoon chopped parsley
Salt and pepper
¼ teaspoon nutmeg
3 tablespoons heavy cream
2 egg yolks

Fresh pasta (see pgs. 50–55)
1 tablespoon vegetable oil
2 tablespoons butter
2½ cups Tomato Sauce (see p. 184)

Combine ricotta, all but 4 tablespoons of Parmesan cheese, prosciutto, parsley, salt and pepper, nutmeg, cream and egg yolks. Mix well.

Prepare fresh pasta and cut according to directions for manicotti. You will need 16 squares. Cook pasta, a few pieces at a time, for 2½ minutes in large pot of salted boiling water to which a tablespoon of vegetable oil has been added. Stir to make sure squares of pasta do not stick together. Drain carefully and cool under cold water. Arrange the pasta squares on a work counter, and place 1½ tablespoons of filling in the center of each square. Bring 2 ends together to slightly overlap, making a roll.

Preheat oven to 350°F. Butter a baking dish large enough to accommodate the manicotti. Spread half of the tomato sauce on bottom of dish. Place manicotti on top, seam side down, and pour more sauce over. Sprinkle with remaining Parmesan cheese. Bake for approximately 10 minutes.

Serves 6-8.

RIPIENO PER PANSOTI
Pansoti Filling

1 pound fresh spinach, or 1 package frozen leaf spinach
  defrosted at room temperature
3 tablespoons butter
1 pound whole-milk ricotta
⅓ teaspoon nutmeg
Salt and pepper to taste
½ tablespoon chopped parsley
3 tablespoons heavy cream
2 egg yolks
1 cup Parmesan
Fresh pasta (see pgs. 50–56)

If using fresh spinach, discard tough stems, wash well in cold
water and drain thoroughly. Boil in salted water 3 minutes.
Drain very well. If using frozen spinach, defrost at room temperature and squeeze free of all water. Sauté fresh or frozen
spinach in butter for 5 minutes. Let cool, reserving butter in
pan. Chop rather fine by hand or in a food processor. Place in
a bowl and blend well with butter from pan, ricotta, nutmeg,
salt and pepper, parsley and heavy cream. Finally, mix in egg
yolks and Parmesan.

Prepare fresh pasta and cut according to directions for
ravioli or pansoti.

To assemble: Follow directions for ravioli (see pgs. 76–77).
Serves 6-8.

PANSOTI ALLA SALSA DI NOCI
Pansoti with Nut Sauce

A typical Ligurian dish, served almost exclusively in Recco, a small village near Genova.

16 tablespoons butter
½ clove garlic, chopped very fine
½ tablespoon chopped parsley
4 fresh basil leaves, chopped fine; or ½ teaspoon dried basil
1 tablespoon pignoli nuts, chopped rather fine
6 ounces shelled walnuts, chopped fine
Freshly ground black pepper to taste
1 pint heavy cream
1 cup grated Parmesan cheese
1 tablespoon vegetable oil
100 ricotta- and spinach-filled pansoti (store-bought), or fresh
    pansoti (see fresh pasta, pgs. 50–56 and Pansoti Filling, p. 67)

In a deep, quart-size pot, melt 12 tablespoons of butter over low flame. Add garlic, parsley and basil, and cook for a few minutes. Add pignoli and walnuts, and stir with a wooden spoon, being careful not to let nuts burn or stick to bottom of pot. Add black pepper to taste. Add heavy cream, and stir until mixture comes to a boil and thickens. Add ½ cup Parmesan cheese, and continue to stir and cook for another 15 minutes. Remove pot from flame.

Bring a gallon of salted water to boil, add tablespoon of oil, then add the pansoti, making sure that they do not stick together. Cooking times: if using homemade, cook 2 minutes; if using store-bought pansoti, cook 8 minutes. Drain carefully to avoid breaking.

In a large frying pan, melt remaining butter, add pansoti to it, and with a wooden spoon turn pansoti until well coated. Gradually add sauce to pan. Heat thoroughly over low flame until pansoti are richly covered with sauce.

Serve piping hot, adding remaining cheese and freshly ground black pepper if desired.

Serves 6-8.

PAGLIA E FIENO
"Straw and Hay" Pasta

Paglia e fieno translates as "straw and hay," describing the
lovely tangle of white and green pasta. (Obviously, the hay in
mind is freshly mown.) I believe this is a Roman dish, created
in the last 10 years, perhaps on the Via Veneto.

12 tablespoons butter
1 clove finely chopped garlic
1½ pounds sweet Italian sausage, removed from casing and
    crumbled
1½ tablespoons chopped parsley
1 teaspoon dried basil leaves, or 4 leaves fresh basil, finely
    chopped
Generous pinch tarragon
Pinch thyme
Pinch oregano
Pinch sage
Pinch nutmeg
Salt and freshly ground pepper to taste
1½ pounds fresh mushrooms
Homemade green and white tagliarini, approximately 1 pound of
    each (see pgs. 50–55), or 1 pound green, 1 pound white dried
    tagliarini
¾ pint heavy cream
½ cup grated Parmesan cheese

Melt 10 tablespoons of butter in a large, deep skillet. Add garlic
and cook without burning. Add sausage meat and cook for 20
minutes while adding herbs, nutmeg, salt and pepper, stirring
frequently. Wash mushrooms thoroughly and slice roughly.
Dry. Add to sausage mixture and cook an additional 15 minutes.
  Bring 2 gallons of salted water to boil, drop both green and
white tagliarini in it. If homemade, cook only 1½ minutes; if
dried, cook 5 minutes. Drain. Make sure sauce is hot. Melt remaining butter in large frying pan, add pasta and sauté lightly
over low flame, then add ½ of the sauce and all of the cream.

Toss well over fire until cream thickens. This process should
not take more than 3 minutes.

Lay pasta in serving platter, top with remaining sauce, serve
with freshly ground pepper and Parmesan cheese.

Serves 6-8.

RIPIENO PER TORTELLINI
Tortellini Filling

6 tablespoons butter
2 boned and skinned breasts of chicken (medium-sized)
1 pound mortadella, in 1 piece
4 slices prosciutto
¼ teaspoon nutmeg
Salt and pepper to taste
½ tablespoon chopped parsley
2 eggs
¾ cup Parmesan
Fresh pasta (see pgs. 50–56)

Melt butter in a frying pan over medium heat, and cook chicken
breasts on both sides until done. Let cool, reserving butter in
pan. Put chicken, mortadella and prosciutto through a meat
grinder or food processor. Transfer to a bowl and blend with
nutmeg, salt and pepper, parsley and butter from frying pan.
When stuffing is totally cooled, thoroughly mix in eggs; add
Parmesan.

Prepare fresh pasta and cut according to directions for
tortellini.

To assemble: After the pasta has been cut into rounds 1½
inches in diameter, place ½ teaspoon of the filling in the center
of each round. Moisten the edges with water. Fold over ½ of
the dough to cover the filling but not quite meet the opposite
edge of dough. Seal the dough where it meets. Wrap these half-
moons around the top of your index finger to form a ring, and
seal the two ends. Dust with sifted floor. Allow to dry for 10-15
minutes before cooking.

TORTELLINI DELLA NONNA

La nonna, "grandmother." Therefore, this is the way grandmother used to make tortellini. That's what the Romans like
to call this dish. But then, all sorts of stories are told about
tortellini. Some even say that their shape is a facsimile of
Venus's very own bellybutton!

200 tortellini (see fresh pasta, pgs. 50–56 and Tortellini Filling
   p. 70)
10 tablespoons butter
½ pint heavy cream
5 thin slices prosciutto, julienned
½ cup cooked peas (canned, frozen or, preferably, fresh)
Freshly ground pepper to taste
1 cup grated Parmesan cheese

Bring to boil 1 gallon salted water. Add tortellini and cook
1½-2 minutes.* Drain gently. In frying pan, melt butter, add
tortellini and mix together thoroughly over low heat with
wooden spoon. Pour in cream, add the prosciutto and continue
to mix well. Add peas, pepper and, finally, cheese. Blend thoroughly. Tortellini must have a rich, creamy look. Serve piping
hot with additional ground pepper and Parmesan cheese.
   Serves 6.

* If using store-bought tortellini, cook 6-8 minutes.

TAGLIARINI VERDI ALLA GHIOTTONA

A Tuscan recipe for thinly cut ribbons of spinach pasta in a sauce fit to please the palate of a *ghiottone*, or glutton.

24 tablespoons butter
½ cup finely chopped onion
¼ cup finely diced carrots
Salt and freshly ground pepper
1 tablespoon chopped parsley
⅛ teaspoon nutmeg
½ pound ground meat, preferably veal, although beef or pork
    might be used
¼ pound chicken livers, cut into ½-inch cubes
1½ tablespoons dry sherry
⅓ cup chicken consommé (see p. 42)
½ cup Cream Sauce (see p. 191)
1 cup Tomato Sauce (see p. 184)
½ tablespoon olive oil
¼ pound prosciutto, shredded, about 1 cup loosely packed
1½ pounds fresh green tagliarini (see pgs. 50–55), although
    spaghettini, spaghetti or dried tagliarini could be used

Heat the butter in a skillet or casserole and add the onion and carrots. When onion becomes translucent, sprinkle with salt and pepper to taste. Cook gently, without browning, about 8 minutes. Add parsley and nutmeg. Add the veal and cook, stirring to break up any lumps. When meat becomes brown, add the chicken livers and dry sherry. Cook, stirring, about 5 minutes; add the chicken consommé. Simmer about 5 minutes. Add cream sauce, simmer 5 minutes more. Add tomato sauce and cook 10 minutes, stirring.

Heat the oil in another skillet and cook prosciutto about 2 minutes, stirring. Add to the sauce and continue to simmer for 20 minutes more.

Bring to boil 1 gallon of salted water. Cook fresh tagliarini 1 minutes; 5-6 minutes if using dried pasta. Drain well. Sauté pasta in large skillet in ½ of the sauce, then pour remaining sauce over pasta in serving platter.

Serves 6-8.

TAGLIARINI (or SPAGHETTINI) CON VERDURE
Pasta with Fresh Vegetables

In Italy it is said that pasta goes with everything. This recipe shows how brilliant it can be with vegetables.

1 small bunch broccoli, cut into florets, leaving 1-inch stem, washed under cold water
10 florets fresh cauliflower, washed
½ pound asparagus, washed
10 tablespoons butter
½ tablespoon chopped parsley
3 fresh basil leaves, chopped; or ½ teaspoon dried basil
Pinch nutmeg
Salt and freshly ground pepper
4 pieces dried mushrooms, presoaked (see p. 13) and chopped
Approximately 1½ pounds homemade tagliarini (see pgs. 50–55), spaghettini or pasta of your choice; or dried tagliarini
½ cup heavy cream
½ cup grated Parmesan cheese

Cook vegetables* in salted boiling water for 3-5 minutes. Drain and run under cold water, making sure not to bruise. When cool, cut into ½-inch pieces.

In a saucepan, melt all but 1½ tablespoons of butter, add the herbs, spices and mushrooms. Cook 5 minutes. Then add the vegetables, and cook an additional 5 minutes.

Bring to boil 1 gallon of salted water. Cook homemade tagliarini 1½ minutes; cook spaghettini 6 minutes; cook short pasta 12 minutes; cook dried tagliarini 5 minutes. Drain.

Melt remaining butter and toss pasta in it. Add vegetable mixture and cream, and stir well. This process should not take more than 3 minutes.

Serve with Parmesan cheese and freshly ground black pepper. Serves 6-8.

---

* Other vegetables in season—zucchini, string beans, peas—can be substituted.

TAGLIARINI VERDI AI QUATTRO FORMAGGI
Green Tagliarini with Four Cheeses

I first tasted this dish at a dinner party in a typical Tuscan farmhouse outside of Lucca. To this day I do not know its true origins.

½ pound butter
¼ teaspoon white pepper
Pinch nutmeg
¼ pound fontina or fonduta cheese, cubed
¼ pound Gorgonzola cheese, crumbled
¼ pound Bel Paese cheese, cubed
1 cup grated Parmesan cheese
1 cup heavy cream
Approximately 1½ pounds homemade tagliarini (see pgs. 50–55) or dried green tagliarini

Melt butter in deep saucepan and season with pepper and nutmeg. Add fontina, Gorgonzola and Bel Paese cheeses, and stir well until all have melted. Then blend in ½ cup Parmesan cheese and all of the cream. Cook 5 minutes, stirring continually with a wire whisk. Bring to boil. Set aside, and keep warm.

Bring 1 gallon of salted water to boil, cook homemade tagliarini 1½ minutes; cook dried tagliarini 5 minutes. Drain well. Toss well with the sauce, and serve with remaining Parmesan cheese and freshly ground pepper.

Serves 6-8.

TAGLIARINI VERDI AL GUANCIALE
Green Tagliarini with Pancetta or Bacon

I invented this dish one rainy evening while at home with Jane and three bunches of beautifully fresh leeks staring at us from the worktable in our kitchen. And we were hungry.

You may choose to substitute another pasta, such as rigatoni, ziti or spaghettini, in this recipe.

2 bunches leeks, all green parts and bottoms cut off, leaving only
   white parts; cut into julienne strips; wash well under cold
   water; dry
6 tablespoons butter
½ teaspoon whole peppercorns
½ teaspoon fresh, chopped Italian parsley
Pinch nutmeg
Salt to taste
¼ pound sliced pancetta, or equivalent strips of bacon, cut into
   ½-inch pieces
1¼ pounds homemade green tagliarini (see pgs. 50–55), or pasta
   of your choice
½ pint heavy cream
½ cup grated Parmesan cheese

Melt 2 tablespoons butter in a deep skillet. Add leeks, parsley, peppercorns, nutmeg and salt. Sauté until leeks are golden and translucent. Set aside.

Sauté pancetta or bacon in frying pan until rather crisp, without letting it become dry or overcrisp. Set aside on paper toweling to absorb grease.

Bring 1 gallon of salted water to boil, drop pasta in it. If tagliarini are homemade, cook 1½ minutes. If you are using rigatoni, or ziti, cook 8-10 minutes. If you are using spaghettini, cook 5 minutes. Drain.

In a large skillet, melt remaining 4 tablespoons butter. Mix pasta in it, blend well and sauté 1 minute. Mix leeks and pancetta with pasta. Sauté 1 minute. Blend in heavy cream and half of the Parmesan cheese; mix well, cook 2 minutes over low heat. Serve with remaining Parmesan and freshly ground pepper on the side.

Serves 6-8.

RIPIENO PER RAVIOLI
Ravioli Filling

½ cup olive oil
1 clove garlic, peeled
1 pound lean beef, such as eye of round
8 tablespoons butter
1 small onion, finely chopped
½ teaspoon nutmeg
Salt and pepper to taste
5 pieces dried mushrooms, presoaked (see p. 13)
1½ tablespoons chopped parsley
1 pound sweet sausage, taken out of casing and crumbled
½ cup red wine
2 tablespoons tomato paste, liquefied with small amount warm
    water
Consommé, if necessary
8 or 9 tender leaves swiss chard, or inner leaves of small head of
    chicory, washed and drained
2 eggs
⅔ cup Parmesan
Fresh pasta (see pgs. 50–56)

Heat oil in a frying pan, add garlic, and brown beef thoroughly. Remove beef from oil and set aside. Discard garlic. Heat 6 tablespoons of butter with oil, add the chopped onions and sauté until golden. Add nutmeg, salt and pepper, mushrooms and parsley, and cook 5 minutes. Add sausage and cook until quite brown. Return beef to pan, cover and cook 5 minutes. Add wine and cook until it evaporates. Pour in tomato paste and cook 30 minutes, stirring continuously. If the mixture becomes too dry, add small amount of consommé.

Let filling cool slightly and put through coarse setting of meat grinder. Then let cool to room temperature.

Boil swiss chard or chicory in salted water for 3 minutes. Drain well. Sauté in remaining 2 tablespoons butter for 5 minutes. Put through grinder, and blend well with rest of filling. Let cool. Thoroughly mix in eggs and Parmesan.

Prepare fresh pasta and cut according to directions for ravioli.

To assemble:* Lay half the strips of pasta on a pastry board or table. Place 1½-teaspoon mounds of filling 1 inch apart down the center of each strip, leaving a border of about ½ inch. Moisten the edges of the dough and the spaces between the fillings with water. Place the remaining strips of pasta on top, and press the moistened dough to seal filling thoroughly. Using a jagged-edged cutting wheel, cut the ravioli into 2- or 2½-inch squares. Dust with sifted flour. Allow to dry for 10 minutes before cooking.

Serves 6-8.

RAVIOLI AU TUCCU
Ravioli with Ragù Sauce

Au tuccu is the Genovese dialect term for "with ragù" or any sauce made with meat or sausage or both. This recipe is truly from the Genovese kitchen. In a moment of nostalgia, any good Genovese away from home might sigh and say: "What I wouldn't do for a dish of *ravioli au tuccu!*"

1 tablespoon vegetable oil

Approximately 70 homemade ravioli (see fresh pasta, pgs. 50–56 and Ravioli Filling, p. 76) or the equivalent in store-bought ravioli

1½ cups Ragù Sauce (see p. 184)

½ cup grated Parmesan cheese

Freshly ground pepper

In a saucepan, warm ragù sauce over low flame.

Bring a gallon of salted water to boil, add the vegetable oil, then the ravioli, making sure they do not stick together. If using homemade, cook 2 minutes; if using store-bought ravioli, cook 8 minutes. Drain carefully to avoid breaking.

Pour ½ cup of ragù sauce in a large skillet. Add the ravioli,

---

* Metal forms for assembling ravioli can be bought in Italian stores or kitchen-equipment shops and will help you make a much more uniform and professional-looking product.

and mix carefully. Heat 1 minute, gently; avoid breaking the ravioli. Arrange ravioli on serving platter, pour remaining ragù over it. Serve with grated Parmesan and pepper.

Serves 6, approximately 10-12 ravioli per person.

GNOCCHI DI PATATE
Potato Gnocchi

An old Roman song for children goes: *Ridi, ridi, che la mamma ha fatto i gnocchi.* ("Laugh, laugh, because mama made gnocchi")—another Italian way of associating food with joy and happiness.

Gnocchi are potato-and-flour dumplings that can be served with a variety of sauces: Butter and Cheese, Fresh Tomato, Bolognese or Ragú.

1½ pounds boiling potatoes
1¾ cups all-purpose flour
Salt to taste
½ tablespoon vegetable oil

Boil potatoes in their skins until done, yet firm. Peel while hot. (Do not run under cold water.) Spread flour on a pasta board. Pass the potatoes through a food mill or potato ricer. Place on the flour. Sprinkle with salt. Start mixing the flour into potatoes a little at a time until the dough is well blended and firm. Knead gently for 6-8 minutes. Sprinkle dough with sifted flour. Cut into several pieces. Roll each piece into a long, sausage-like shape, ½ inch in diameter. Then cut into 1-inch pieces. Dust again with sifted flour. Let rest 5 minutes.

To form gnocchi: Using your thumb, gently roll pieces down the inside of a table fork, so that they curl and are imprinted with the tines.

Bring to boil a large pot of salted water, add oil. Quickly drop gnocchi, one by one, into the pot. Stir water with a wooden spoon so that gnocchi will not stick together. In a few seconds gnocchi will come to the surface of water. Let them cook 1 more minute. Strain by using strainer-skimmer. Lay gnocchi on serving platter in which you may pour sauce of your choice:

BUTTER AND CHEESE: Melt 4 tablespoons of butter, mix well with gnocchi and serve with Parmesan.

FRESH TOMATO (see p. 184): Heat 2 cups of sauce, mix well with gnocchi and serve with Parmesan.

BÓLOGNESE (see p. 186): Heat 1½ cups sauce, mix well with gnocchi and serve with Parmesan.

RAGÙ (see p. 184): Heat 1½ cups sauce, mix well with gnocchi and serve with Parmesan.

Serves 6.

SPAGHETTINI ALLE VONGOLE
Spaghettini with Clam Sauce (Red or White)

4 dozen fresh, medium-sized clams
3 tablespoons olive oil
1 teaspoon chopped garlic
½ tablespoon chopped parsley
Freshly ground black pepper to taste
Generous pinch oregano
Pinch crushed red pepper
1 pound spaghettini

For red sauce:
1 cup Italian peeled tomatoes, drained

WHITE SAUCE
Wash clams thoroughly under cold water, and open over mixing bowl so as not to lose any juice. (Clams may also be opened by steaming lightly.) Scoop clams out carefully and discard shells.

Heat oil in saucepan and sauté garlic until golden. Add parsley, pepper, oregano and crushed red pepper. Then add clams, without juice, and cook 5 minutes. (If you have steamed clams open, cook for just 2 or 3 minutes.) Remove from heat to avoid a flare-up of oil and add clam juice. Return pan to heat and cook 2 more minutes.

RED SAUCE

Follow directions for white clam sauce through the point when herbs and seasonings are added. Then, add tomatoes. Cook 10 minutes. Add clams, cook 5 minutes (or 2 or 3 minutes if clams have been steamed), and finally add clam juice, *off heat*. Return pan to heat and cook an additional 2 minutes.

SPAGHETTINI

Cook spaghettini in 4 quarts salted boiling water for 4 or 5 minutes. Drain well. If serving white sauce, keep some of the hot cooking water and add 2 tablespoons of it to serving dish, along with the spaghettini. If serving red sauce, do not add water.

Pour hot sauce over spaghettini and serve with additional freshly ground pepper and crushed red pepper. Grated cheese is optional.

Serves 6.

SPAGHETTINI AL SALTO

A rather whimsical Via Veneto invention, but what tasty results!

8 medium tomatoes, cut into chunks
⅔ cup olive oil
3 fresh basil leaves, chopped coarsely, or ½ teaspoon dried basil
1 teaspoon red wine vinegar
Salt and pepper
1 pound imported spaghettini
½ cup grated Parmesan cheese

Toss tomatoes, oil, basil and vinegar together as if tossing a salad. Salt and pepper to taste. Let it marinate for at least 1 hour at room temperature.

Cook spaghettini in salted boiling water for 5 minutes, or until *al dente*. Drain well.

Combine sauce and spaghettini, and serve with Parmesan cheese.

Serves 6.

SPAGHETTINI CARBONARA
Spaghettini with Bacon, Egg and Cheese

This dish got its name from the freshly ground black pepper showered over the pasta, resembling "coal dust." The word *carbonara* derives from *carbone,* meaning "coal."

¼ pound pancetta (Italian bacon)
1 pound imported Italian spaghettini
6 tablespoons butter
½ tablespoon white wine
2 egg yolks
⅓ cup heavy cream
¾ cup grated Parmesan cheese
Salt and freshly ground black pepper

Cut the pancetta slices in thirds and cook to a crisp in a skillet.

Cook spaghettini in 4 quarts salted boiling water for 4-5 minutes and drain. Combine butter and wine in a large frying pan over medium flame, and let the wine reduce quickly. Place spaghettini in pan and cook for 2 minutes, tossing to coat well.

Add egg yolks and cream. Mix quickly so that the eggs do not scramble. Add ½ cup Parmesan cheese and mix well again. Season generously with freshly ground pepper. This procedure should take only 2 minutes. The crisp pancetta should be mixed into the pasta. Serve with remaining Parmesan cheese and additional freshly ground black pepper.

Serves 6.

SPAGHETTINI AL PESTO
Spaghettini with Basil Sauce

The most famous, most ingenious of all the recipes of the
Genovese kitchen. There are many versions of the pesto sauce.
Most of those used in this country overlook two ingredients
found in authentic Genovese recipes—heavy cream and Pre-
scinsoa cheese. The latter is not available here, but cream
cheese makes a reasonable substitute.

1½ cups (approximately) Pesto Sauce (see p. 190), at room
    temperature for 1 hour
1 pound spaghettini
2 tablespoons butter
½ cup grated pecorino cheese

Cook spaghettini in 1 gallon boiling salted water. Drain well,
reserving ¼ cup of the hot cooking water.
    Place butter in a serving dish with 3 tablespoons of pesto
sauce. Mix in spaghettini and the hot water. Add remaining
sauce. Serve piping hot with pecorino cheese and freshly ground
black pepper.
    Serves 6.

FUSILLI CON PESTO E PATATE
Pasta with Pesto and Potatoes

1 cup (approximately) Pesto Sauce (see p. 190), at room
    temperature for 1 hour
¾ pound potatoes*
4 tablespoons butter
1 pound fusilli (imported)
½ cup grated pecorino cheese

* A variation on the above recipe is to use fresh string beans instead of potatoes:
Trim and wash under cold water ¾ pound of fresh string beans. Cook in salted,
boiling water for 10-12 minutes. Drain. Sauté in 2 tablespoons of butter for 5 minutes. Keep warm. Then follow recipe as above.

Peel potatoes, wash under cold water, cut into ½-inch cubes.
Cook in salted water, leaving very *al dente*. Drain. Melt 2
tablespoons of butter in a frying pan. Sauté potatoes for about
10 minutes. Keep warm.

Cook fusilli in 1 gallon boiling salted water for 8 minutes.
Drain well, reserving ¼ cup of the hot cooking water. Place
remaining 2 tablespoons of butter in serving dish with 3 tablespoons of pesto sauce. Mix in fusilli, hot water and potatoes.
Add remaining sauce. Serve piping hot with pecorino cheese
and freshly ground black pepper.

Serves 6.

PERCIATELLI ALL'AMATRICIANA
Perciatelli Amatrice Style

This dish is named for a small town outside of Rome called
Amatrice, well known for its pork products. This is a rather
spicy dish since it is usually served with red pepper.

1½ tablespoons butter
1 tablespoon olive oil
¼ teaspoon chopped garlic
½ tablespoon chopped parsley
Pinch sage
¼ teaspoon crushed red pepper
½ teaspoon salt
¼ teaspoon black pepper
¼ pound pancetta (Italian bacon), sliced rather thickly and cut
    into chunks
1 35-ounce can (2½ cups) peeled Italian tomatoes, drained
1 pound imported Italian perciatelli
¼ cup pecorino cheese

Melt 1 tablespoon butter and oil in a saucepan and add garlic,
parsley, sage, red pepper, and salt and pepper. When garlic
turns golden, add pancetta. Cook for 6 minutes over medium

flame. Then add tomatoes, breaking them up, and simmer for 20 minutes.

Cook perciatelli in 1 gallon boiling salted water for 8 minutes. Drain. Combine ½ tablespoon butter and 3 tablespoons sauce in a large frying pan. Add perciatelli and mix well. Pour remaining sauce over pasta and mix well again. Serve with pecorino cheese and more crushed red pepper.

Serves 6.

RIGATONI CON ZUCCHINI
Macaroni with Zucchini

Venetian? Tuscan? Roman or Bolognese? Whatever the origins, the most delectable blend of a fresh vegetable, prosciutto, butter, cream and that sainted Parmigiano cheese.

6 medium-sized zucchini
12 tablespoons butter
1 pound rigatoni (preferably imported)
½ pint heavy cream
6 slices prosciutto, julienned
Freshly ground black pepper (7-8 mill turns)
1 cup grated Parmesan cheese

Wash zucchini thoroughly under cold running water, chop off ends, then cut each lengthwise into 4 strips. Dice strips. Sauté in 4 tablespoons of butter in a large skillet, adding salt to taste. Cooking time is 15 minutes. Set aside.

Bring a large pot of salted water to a boil, drop in rigatoni, cook 12 minutes, then drain. Melt remaining butter in a large skillet, add drained rigatoni and toss well with the butter. Add, one at a time, cream, zucchini and prosciutto, mixing well after each addition. Finally, add pepper and ¾ cup of cheese, and mix thoroughly until rigatoni are completely coated and cream has thickened considerably.

Turn out piping hot mixture into a large, warm serving dish. Serve immediately, sprinkling each portion with remaining cheese.

Serves 6.

RIGATONI ALLA VIAREGGINA

Ah, Viareggio! Carnevale, the incomparable pine tree gardens, and the dusty, romantic Buffet della Stazione where I first ate this particular pasta. It's all in the past . . . *purtroppo.*

3 tablespoons olive oil
½ teaspoon chopped garlic
4 filets of anchovies
Pinch oregano
Pinch thyme
3 fresh basil leaves, chopped; or ½ teaspoon dry basil
1 tablespoon chopped parsley
Freshly ground black pepper
1 7-ounce can Italian tuna in olive oil, undrained*
1 18-ounce can imported Italian peeled tomatoes, undrained
1½ pounds imported rigatoni
1 tablespoon butter
½ cup grated Parmesan cheese

Heat oil in saucepan and sauté garlic over low heat without browning. Add anchovies and cook until reduced to a paste. Add all herbs, pepper and tuna (broken up with a fork). Cook 5 minutes. Add peeled tomatoes, also broken up, and gradually add the juice, a little at a time. Cook over medium heat for 25 minutes. Set aside.

Cook rigatoni in boiling salted water for 10-12 minutes. Drain well.

Melt butter in large frying pan and toss rigatoni in it. Then add the sauce and mix very well over low heat, about 3 minutes. Serve with Parmesan cheese and freshly ground black pepper.
Serves 6.

---

* Drain if using American tuna.

PENNE ALL'ARRABBIATA

Penne all'Arrabbiata—a typical Roman dish—actually means "in a mad style." Romans use red pepper on it. Served mainly at trattorie in Trastevere.

¼ cup olive oil
4 tablespoons butter
½ teaspoon chopped garlic
1 pound Italian sweet sausage, removed from casing
½ tablespoon chopped parsley
Generous pinch dried basil, or 2-3 fresh leaves, chopped
Generous pinch oregano
Pinch thyme
½ teaspoon crushed red pepper
2 tablespoons dry red wine
1 35-ounce can Italian peeled tomatoes, drained
Salt and pepper
1 15-ounce can artichoke hearts in brine
1 pound imported Italian penne
½ cup grated pecorino cheese
½ cup grated Parmesan cheese

Heat oil and melt ½ the butter in saucepan; cook garlic until golden. Add sausage meat in small chunks. Stirring continuously, sauté over medium flame until it begins to brown. Then add all the herbs and crushed red pepper. Cook an additional 5 minutes. Still stirring, add wine and cook over high flame until wine evaporates. Add tomatoes and salt and pepper, and cook 20 minutes. Set sauce aside.

Cut artichoke hearts in half and drain. Place in dish and salt lightly. Leave out ½ hour at room temperature.

Cook penne in 1 gallon boiling salted water for 10 minutes. Drain. Melt remaining butter in baking dish and add some sauce. Combine well with penne off the flame. Begin to sprinkle in pecorino cheese while slowly adding more sauce, followed by ½ of the Parmesan cheese. Then garnish whole dish with artichoke hearts. Pour remaining sauce over, and cover with remaining cheese. Bake in oven preheated to 350°F approximately 8 minutes.

Serves 6.

PENNE ALLA ZAMPOGNARA

The *zampognari*, dressed in sheepskins, descend on Rome from Abruzzi at Christmastime to play the traditional holiday tunes on their bagpipes, (*zampogne*). Someone must have thought it appropriate to dedicate a pasta to them.

1 pound Italian sweet sausage
Salt and freshly ground pepper to taste
¼ cup olive oil
3½ cups Tomato Sauce (see p. 184)
6 pieces dried mushrooms, presoaked (see p. 13)
½ pound whole-milk ricotta
⅓ cup grated pecorino cheese
⅔ cup grated Parmesan cheese
1 egg yolk
1 pound imported penne

Take sausage out of casing, sprinkle with salt and pepper, and form into small balls. Heat oil in a skillet over low flame, cook until done about 10 minutes. Drain on paper toweling. Set aside.

Heat tomato sauce in saucepan over low flame, add mushrooms and sausage balls, cook 15 minutes. Set aside, and keep warm.

In a mixing bowl, blend ricotta, pecorino and ⅓ cup Parmesan (reserve the rest for later). Blend in egg yolk. Set aside.

Bring 1 gallon of salted water to boil, cook penne 10-12 minutes. Drain. Heat penne in 1 cup of sause in a frying pan. Lay pasta in serving dish. Pour remaining sauce over it. Top with ricotta mixture. Serve with remaining Parmesan and the pepper mill.

Serves 6.

PENNE ALLA LUCCHESE
Pasta, Lucchese Style

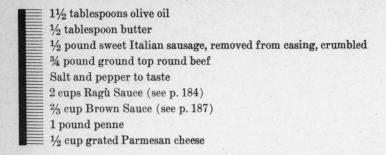

1½ tablespoons olive oil
½ tablespoon butter
½ pound sweet Italian sausage, removed from casing, crumbled
¾ pound ground top round beef
Salt and pepper to taste
2 cups Ragù Sauce (see p. 184)
⅔ cup Brown Sauce (see p. 187)
1 pound penne
½ cup grated Parmesan cheese

Heat oil and butter in a frying pan, add sausage, cook until brown. Add ground beef and cook for 20 minutes, turning often. Add salt and pepper. Heat ragú in a saucepan. Add sausage and beef mixture, cook 5 minutes. Add brown sauce, mix well, cook 10 minutes. Set aside.

Bring to boil 1 gallon of salted water. Cook penne 10-12 minutes. Drain well. In a large skillet, heat penne in sauce, mixing thoroughly. Serve with Parmesan cheese and the pepper mill.

Serves 6.

ORECCHIETTE CINQUE TERRE

Orecchiette is pasta shaped like small hats the size of a nickel. Why it was ever called *orecchiette* or "little ears," I'll never know! The "Cinque Terre" sauce is one of my improvisations.

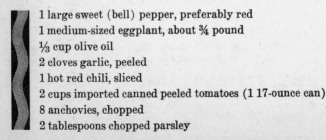

1 large sweet (bell) pepper, preferably red
1 medium-sized eggplant, about ¾ pound
⅓ cup olive oil
2 cloves garlic, peeled
1 hot red chili, sliced
2 cups imported canned peeled tomatoes (1 17-ounce can)
8 anchovies, chopped
2 tablespoons chopped parsley

1 tablespoon chopped fresh basil, 2 teaspoons dried basil
¼ cup (about 24) pitted olives, preferably imported (Gaeta)
1 pound orecchiette or other pasta
⅓ cup grated Parmesan cheese

Preheat oven to 400°F. Place the sweet pepper on a sheet of aluminum foil and bake 30 minutes or until the pepper blisters and starts to blacken. Let cool. Trim the ends of the eggplant. Cut the eggplant into ½-inch cubes.

Heat the oil; add the garlic and sliced red chili. Cook until garlic and chili are browned. Remove and discard garlic and chili. Add the eggplant and cook 10 minutes.

Drain the tomatoes but save the pulp and the juice. There should be about 1 cup each of pulp and juice. Add the pulp to the oil and eggplant, cook 15 minutes.

Add the anchovies. Cook, stirring constantly, about 8 minutes. Add the parsley, basil, olives and the reserved tomato juice. Cook 5-10 minutes.

Peel, core and seed the sweet pepper. Cut it into ½-inch cubes. Add the pepper to the sauce. Cover and cook about 10 minutes over low heat, stirring occasionally.

Boil orecchiette until *al dente,* approximately 8 minutes. Drain. Heat pasta with the sauce for approximately 3 minutes, or until pasta is well coated. Heat. Serve with Parmesan cheese.

Serves 6.

PASTA MANTECATA

A blend of velvety sauce and pasta. A delicious offering from Tuscany.

8 tablespoons butter
½ cup dried mushrooms, presoaked (see p. 13), cut in coarse pieces
¾ cup fresh peas, shelled and washed; or frozen peas, defrosted at room temperature
Salt and freshly ground pepper to taste
¼ pound prosciutto, ham or mortadella, julienned*
⅓ cup Brown Sauce (see p. 187)
¾ cup heavy cream
Pinch of nutmeg
¾ cup Parmesan cheese
1 pound pasta of your choice

Melt butter in frying pan large enough to accommodate all ingredients. Sauté mushrooms 3 minutes. Add peas, sauté 2 minutes. Add salt and pepper to taste. Add prosciutto, ham or mortadella and sauté for 3 minutes. Add brown sauce, cook 3 minutes. Add heavy cream and cook 3 minutes. Sprinkle nutmeg over. Add ½ cup Parmesan cheese and blend thoroughly. Set aside.

Bring to boil 1 gallon of salted water. Cook pasta: spaghettini, 6 minutes; short pasta (macaroni), 10-12 minutes; homemade fresh pasta, 2 minutes. Drain. Heat pasta in sauce in the same pan. This should take no more than 1½ minutes. Serve with remaining Parmesan cheese and pepper mill. Serves 6.

---

* Boned and skinned breast of chicken can be used in place of prosciutto, ham or mortadella. If so, you will have to cook chicken beforehand in butter (making sure not to overcook), then dice chicken rather small, and follow recipe as above.

Risotti e Polenta

RISOTTO ALLA MILANESE
Saffron Rice

Another claim to fame of the Milanese, along with their
centuries-old, still unfinished Cathedral, their beautiful city
and their knack for making money.

½ pound butter
½ small onion, finely sliced
White pepper
1 tablespoon dry white wine
1 pound imported Italian rice (Arborio)
10-12 pieces dried Italian mushrooms, presoaked (see p. 13) and
    roughly chopped
5 cups consommé, beef or chicken (see p. 000)
¼ teaspoon saffron, mixed in small amount of consommé
¾ cup grated Parmesan cheese

Melt butter in a large pan and sauté onion until golden. Add
pepper to taste. Add wine and cook until it evaporates. Add
rice and cook 5-6 minutes. Stir in mushrooms, and then add
consommé, ½ cup at a time, stirring continuously with a wooden
spoon. When rice is nearly done (*al dente*), add saffron liquid.*
Continue stirring and then add ½ cup Parmesan cheese. The
finished rice should be a marvelous yellow color.

Place in a serving dish, and serve with remaining Parmesan
cheese and freshly ground black pepper.

Serves 6.

RISOTTO ALLA PIEMONTESE
Rice with Sausage and Truffles

Just as famous as the Risotto Alla Milanese, and a lot more
expensive to make. This dish has the same ingredients as the
Milanese, with the following differences:

---

* The entire process of cooking the rice shouldn't take longer than 25 minutes.
The saffron should be added during the last 10 minutes of cooking.

Omit saffron

Add ½ pound Italian sweet sausage, removed from casing and
   broken into chunks

Pinch sage

2 bay leaves

Fresh white truffles (optional and **very expensive**)

Cook chunks of sausage with sage and bay leaves until quite
well done. Drain of all fat. Remove bay leaves and mix sausage
in with rice when it is nearly done. Continue to stir and cook
for another 5 minutes, until *al dente*.

    Spoon the rice into a serving dish or individual dishes. Shave
the truffle over the rice.

    Serves 6.

RISOTTO ALLA PESCATORE
Rice Fisherman Style

⅓ cup olive oil

12 tablespoons butter

½ small onion, finely sliced

½ teaspoon chopped garlic

6 anchovy filets

10 pieces imported dried mushrooms, presoaked (see p. 13) and
   roughly chopped

1 tablespoon chopped parsley

1 teaspoon dried basil, or 4 fresh leaves, chopped

¼ teaspoon dried tarragon leaves, or 4-5 fresh leaves, chopped

Pinch crushed red pepper

Freshly ground black pepper (8-10 generous mill turns)

½ tablespoon small capers

1 17-ounce can peeled Italian tomatoes, undrained

1½ pounds small fresh shrimp, shelled, deveined and washed

1 dozen fresh clams, washed under cold water and opened, saving
   juice*

1 pound Arborio Italian rice, washed and drained

4 cups consommé, chicken or beef (see p. 42)

½ cup grated Parmesan cheese

* You can steam clams open if you prefer.

Heat oil and 4 tablespoons butter in pan and sauté onion over medium flame until transparent. Combine garlic and anchovy filets and cook 3 minutes. (Three-quarters teaspoon of anchovy paste may be used in place of the filets.) Add mushrooms and cook 5 minutes. Add herbs, crushed red pepper, freshly ground black pepper and capers, and cook 2 minutes. Add peeled tomatoes and cook 20 minutes. Add shrimp and clams, and cook 6 minutes. Remove from flame and mix in clam juice. Set aside.

Melt remaining butter in pan. Add rice, and while stirring with a wooden spoon, cook 6 minutes. Add consommé a little at a time, stirring continuously, until rice is cooked *al dente* or approximately 20 minutes. It should absorb the consommé and be almost dry. Place piping hot rice in a serving dish. Pour some heated sauce over rice and mix well. Then pour remaining sauce over. Serve with Parmesan cheese, and pass the pepper mill.

Serves 6.

POLENTA
Corn Meal

 1 pound polenta (if using American corn meal, see p. 10)
1½ teaspoons salt
2 tablespoons butter

Bring 2 quarts of water to a boil in a heavy stockpot. Add salt. Dribble in polenta a little at a time, stirring continuously with a wooden spoon, making sure there are no lumps. As soon as polenta thickens, which should take 35 minutes, mix in butter. Leave for 5 minutes off the flame. Pour into a flat baking dish.

Serve as a main dish in any of the following ways:

POLENTA CON GORGONZOLA
Polenta with Gorgonzola

2 tablespoons butter
¼ pound Gorgonzola cheese, crusts removed, broken into pieces
½ cup grated Parmesan cheese

Preheat oven to 350°F. Combine polenta, butter and Gorgonzola. Bake in preheated oven for 4-5 minutes. Serve with grated Parmesan on the side.

Serves 6.

POLENTA CON SALSA DI FUNGHI
Polenta with Mushroom Sauce

4 tablespoons butter
½ cup dried mushrooms, presoaked (see p. 13) and coarsely chopped
¼ tablespoon chopped parsley
¼ teaspoon chopped garlic
3½ cups Tomato Sauce (see p. 184)
½ cup grated Parmesan cheese

Melt butter in saucepan, and sauté mushrooms, parsley and garlic for 6 minutes. Mix in tomato sauce, and cook over a low flame for 10 minutes. Set aside and keep warm. Pour sauce over hot polenta, and top with Parmesan cheese. Serve with freshly ground pepper.

Serves 6.

POLENTA E LUGANEGA
Polenta and Sausage

A typical Venetian dish.

1 pound luganega sausage, cut in 3-inch pieces
¼ cup olive oil
2 cloves garlic, peeled
½ tablespoon rosemary
Pinch oregano
¼ tablespoon chopped parsley
Pinch red pepper
Salt and pepper
1 tablespoon dry red wine
3½ cups Tomato Sauce (see p. 184)
6 pieces dried mushrooms, presoaked (see p. 13)
½ cup grated Parmesan cheese

Combine sausage with oil, garlic, herbs and red pepper, and season with salt and pepper. Cook in oven preheated to 350°F for 10 minutes. Add wine, and cook another 5 minutes. Remove sausage and garlic, and strain liquid. Discard garlic. Replace sausage and strained liquid in pan, add tomato sauce and mushrooms. Cook 10 minutes. Set aside and keep warm. Cook polenta according to recipe on page 94.

Pour sauce over hot polenta, and arrange sausage around it on serving platter. Serve with Parmesan cheese.

Serves 6-8.

POLENTA FRITTA

Fried Polenta

Cut polenta into ½-inch slices, fry to a crisp in 1 cup of vegetable oil, and then serve in lieu of bread—as the Venetians do—with some dishes. It can also be served in the form of polenta croutons; or used as a breakfast cereal simply by frying, sprinkling with sugar while very hot, and then pouring milk over it. It makes yet another breakfast dish if fried and spread with butter or jam.

Main Courses

Vitello

Veal

SCALOPPINE LOCANDA MONTIN

At Locanda Montin in Venice—a restaurant located behind the Accademia boat station—this dish is served with slices of fried polenta,* an intriguing *ambiente,* lots of laughs, and a great many interesting patrons.

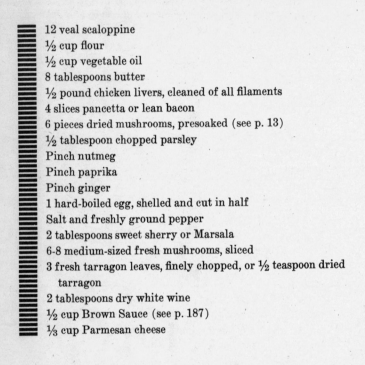

12 veal scaloppine
½ cup flour
½ cup vegetable oil
8 tablespoons butter
½ pound chicken livers, cleaned of all filaments
4 slices pancetta or lean bacon
6 pieces dried mushrooms, presoaked (see p. 13)
½ tablespoon chopped parsley
Pinch nutmeg
Pinch paprika
Pinch ginger
1 hard-boiled egg, shelled and cut in half
Salt and freshly ground pepper
2 tablespoons sweet sherry or Marsala
6-8 medium-sized fresh mushrooms, sliced
3 fresh tarragon leaves, finely chopped, or ½ teaspoon dried
    tarragon
2 tablespoons dry white wine
½ cup Brown Sauce (see p. 187)
⅓ cup Parmesan cheese

Dust each veal scaloppine lightly with flour. Heat oil in a large frying pan until very hot, and in single layers sauté veal quickly on both sides. Transfer carefully to a warm platter. Set aside.

Melt 3 tablespoons butter in a frying pan and brown chicken livers lightly 3-4 minutes. Add pancetta or bacon, and cook over low flame until half done, approximately 10 minutes. Add dry mushrooms, parsley, spices and the egg, and season with salt and pepper. Stirring constantly, add Marsala wine or sherry, and cook 10 minutes. Set aside to cool.

---

* If you should want to serve this dish with fried polenta, see page 94.

Melt remaining butter in a saucepan and sauté sliced mushrooms and tarragon for 5 minutes. Add white wine and cook until wine evaporates, which should take less than 1 minute. Add brown sauce and cook 5 minutes. Pour into a large baking dish and arrange scaloppine over sauce. Bake in a preheated 350°F oven for 8 minutes, turning veal once.

Meanwhile, put chicken liver mixture through a very fine grinder or food mixer. Mix in cheese, and blend well with a wire whisk until it has the consistency of a pâté.

To serve, place a teaspoon of liver pâté atop each slice of veal scaloppine. Spoon sauce over.

Serves 6.

Serve with a light red wine, such as a good Valpolicella or a Rosatello del Garda.

SCALOPPINE TANCREDI

In memory of my history professor, Signor Tommaso Tancredi.

12 veal scaloppine
½ cup flour
½ cup vegetable oil
16 tablespoons butter
24 large mushrooms, washed thoroughly under cold water, and
    with caps and stems separated; slice stems
1 clove garlic, peeled
Pinch nutmeg
Pinch ginger
Pinch paprika
1 tablespoon chopped parsley
¾ cup Marsala
½ cup Brown Sauce (see p. 187)
¼ pound sliced prosciutto
Salt and pepper to taste

Dust each veal scaloppine lightly with flour. Heat oil in a large frying pan and brown scaloppine quickly on both sides in a

single layer. Transfer carefully to a warm platter. In a preheated 350°F oven, bake mushroom caps in a pan with 4 tablespoons of butter for 10 minutes. Melt remaining butter in frying
pan. Add garlic, let it brown over medium heat, and then discard it. Add spices and parsley. Cook 5 minutes. Add sliced
mushroom stems and cook another 5 minutes. Add veal and
cook again quickly on both sides. Add Marsala and let it reduce,
which should take 3 minutes. Then add brown sauce and cook
10 minutes. Finally, add prosciutto and cook 3 minutes. Taste
for seasoning.

Place scaloppine in a serving dish, garnish with mushroom
caps, and pour sauce over.

Serves 6.

Serve with Gattinara or Barolo wine.

SCALOPPINE SALSA BOCUSE

This sauce has nothing to do with the Grand Chef Paul Bocuse.
I named it after the death-defying aerial cyclist Maurice Bocuse,
who was unemployed when I met him at Forte dei Marmi in
Tuscany.

12 veal scaloppine
½ cup flour
½ cup vegetable oil
8 tablespoons butter
3 shallots, peeled and finely minced
1½ teaspoons Dijon mustard
1 teaspoon A-1 Sauce
1 teaspoon Worcestershire Sauce
4 leaves fresh tarragon, or 4 leaves tarragon preserved in
    vinegar, chopped
½ tablespoon chopped parsley
Pinch nutmeg
Pinch cayenne pepper
Pinch paprika
Salt and freshly ground pepper
¼ teaspoon chopped garlic
½ cup Brown Sauce (see p. 187)

Shells of 4 shrimp (shrimp are not used in this dish)
½ cup dry white wine
1½ tablespoons cognac
½ cup heavy cream

Dust each veal scaloppine lightly with flour. Heat oil in large frying pan until very hot, and brown veal quickly on both sides in a single layer. Transfer carefully to a warm platter. Set aside.

Melt butter in a saucepan and cook shallots for 5 minutes over low flame. Add mustard, A-1 and Worcestershire sauces. Mix well. Add herbs, spices, salt and pepper, garlic and brown sauce. Cook 10 minutes. Add shrimp shells and wine, cook until wine evaporates—or about 5 or 6 minutes. Then put sauce through a fine wire strainer. Return to saucepan. Add cognac and cook 3 minutes. Fold in cream, blend well with wire whisk so that sauce does not separate. Cook 6 minutes.

Pour some of the sauce into a large skillet. Arrange scaloppine over the sauce, pour the rest of the sauce over them. Cook over a medium flame 5-6 minutes, turning frequently, until scaloppine are well coated.

Serves 6.

Serve with a well-chilled white wine such as Frascati or a good Soave.

SCALOPPINE DEL RE
The King's Scaloppine

To suit the taste of a King? Kings and royalty are always
dragged in at some time or other in the Italian kitchen.

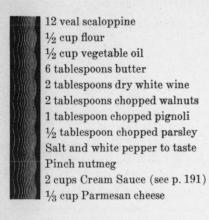

12 veal scaloppine
½ cup flour
½ cup vegetable oil
6 tablespoons butter
2 tablespoons dry white wine
2 tablespoons chopped walnuts
1 tablespoon chopped pignoli
½ tablespoon chopped parsley
Salt and white pepper to taste
Pinch nutmeg
2 cups Cream Sauce (see p. 191)
⅓ cup Parmesan cheese

Dust each veal scaloppine lightly with flour. Heat oil in large
frying pan until very hot and brown veal quickly on both sides,
in a single layer. Transfer carefully to a warm platter.

Heat 2 tablespoons butter and the wine in a saucepan, add
the nuts, parsley, salt and pepper, and nutmeg. Cook 8 minutes.
Add nut mixture to cream sauce, blend well, heat 5 minutes. Set
aside.

Melt remaining butter in baking pan. Arrange veal scaloppine in pan and cover with cream sauce. Sprinkle cheese over
top. Bake for 10 minutes in a preheated 350°F. oven.

Serves 6.

Serve with a well-chilled white Brolio Chianti or a Verdicchio.

SCALOPPINE BENTIVOGLIO

The name "Bentivoglio" always reminds me of some noble
Florentine family that I never met and, perhaps, that never
existed. But, the sound of it is so pleasing, so *signorile*.

8 tablespoons butter
4 fresh tarragon leaves, chopped, or ½ teaspoon dried tarragon
1 tablespoon parsley, chopped
Salt and freshly ground pepper to taste
2 pounds fresh mushrooms, washed, sliced
½ cup dry white wine
1½ cups Brown Sauce (see p. 187)
6 slices Italian bread, ½-inch thick
1 medium clove garlic, finely chopped
1¼ cups vegetable oil
¼ cup Parmesan cheese
6 paper-thin slices mozzarella cheese
12 slices veal scaloppine
½ cup flour

Heat butter to sizzling in a large, deep saucepan but do not let brown. Add tarragon, parsley, salt and pepper, cook 5 minutes. Add mushrooms, and cook over low flame for approximately 10 minutes. Add wine and continue cooking until wine is reduced—about 5 minutes—then add brown sauce, cook 15 minutes. Remove from fire and set aside.

Place bread slices in baking pan. Mix garlic in ¼ cup of oil and spread evenly over bread slices, then sprinkle with Parmesan cheese and top each bread slice with a slice of mozzarella. Place pan in a preheated 300°F oven. Cook until cheese melts, then remove, set aside and keep warm.

Meantime, dust veal slices lightly in flour. Heat remaining oil in large skillet and sauté veal, in a single layer, until golden. Remove from oil, drain and place in previously prepared sauce. Cook over low fire for 8 minutes.

Arrange hot bread slices on platter, cover each with 2 veal slices, and pour sauce over entire dish.

Serves 6.

Serve with a full-bodied red wine such as a Chianti Riserva or a Barbera.

SCALOPPINE MARENGO

Scaloppine Marengo was apparently a favorite dish of Napoleon during the Italian campaign.

12 veal scaloppine
½ cup flour
½ cup vegetable oil
8 tablespoons butter
½ teaspoon chopped garlic
1 tablespoon chopped parsley
Pinch thyme
Pinch oregano
2 leaves fresh basil, chopped coarsely, or ½ teaspoon dried basil
Pinch nutmeg
Salt and pepper
1 tablespoon tomato paste
1 cup chicken consommé (see p. 42)
5 or 6 pieces dried mushrooms, presoaked (see p. 13)
8 fresh mushrooms, washed and sliced
¼ cup dry red wine
2 cups canned Italian peeled tomatoes, drained

Dust each veal scaloppine lightly with flour. Heat oil in large frying pan until very hot, and sauté scaloppine quickly on both sides in a single layer. Transfer carefully to a warm platter.

Melt the butter in a saucepan and cook the garlic for 3 minutes over low heat. Add the herbs, spices, tomato paste and ⅓ cup consommé, and mix well. Cook 5 minutes. Add dried and fresh mushrooms and wine. Cook 10 minutes, stirring constantly. If sauce seems to be getting too thick, add more consommé. Add peeled tomatoes and cook 25 minutes.

Allow sauce to cool, pour into a large baking dish and arrange the veal scaloppine in the sauce. Bake in a preheated 350°F. oven for 5-6 minutes. Spoon sauce over scaloppine and serve.
Serves 6.
Serve with a red wine—Barbaresco or a good Bardolino.

SCALOPPINE SICILIANA

When I owned the Portofino Restaurant in New York's Green-wich Village, I employed a young Sicilian dishwasher, quite ordinary in appearance but with the most arrogant stare one could imagine. Although he was rather slight in build, he could easily intimidate a much larger person with his cold look. He wanted to be a cook and he intimidated me to the extent that I felt I had to eat anything he might make especially for me. He would serve the dish himself and then proceed to watch me intently while I ate it. Sometimes a dish would be delicious, as in the case of these scaloppine. At other times, it would be a disaster, but I would eat it anyway. I call this dish "Siciliana" in honor of his birthplace.

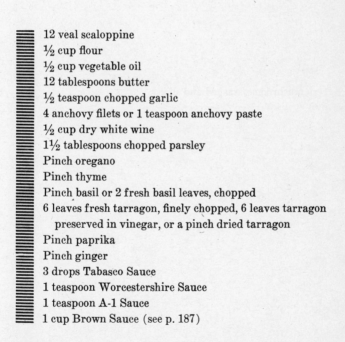

12 veal scaloppine
½ cup flour
½ cup vegetable oil
12 tablespoons butter
½ teaspoon chopped garlic
4 anchovy filets or 1 teaspoon anchovy paste
½ cup dry white wine
1½ tablespoons chopped parsley
Pinch oregano
Pinch thyme
Pinch basil or 2 fresh basil leaves, chopped
6 leaves fresh tarragon, finely chopped, 6 leaves tarragon
    preserved in vinegar, or a pinch dried tarragon
Pinch paprika
Pinch ginger
3 drops Tabasco Sauce
1 teaspoon Worcestershire Sauce
1 teaspoon A-1 Sauce
1 cup Brown Sauce (see p. 187)

Dust each veal scaloppine lightly with flour. Heat oil in a large frying pan until very hot and sauté scaloppine quickly on both sides in a single layer. Transfer carefully to a warm platter.

Melt butter in frying pan and cook garlic for 3 minutes,

making sure it does not burn. Add anchovy filets and cook until
they reach the consistency of a paste (or just add anchovy
paste). Add wine, herbs, spices and bottled sauces. Cook until
wine evaporates—about 5-6 minutes. Add brown sauce gradually and cook for 10 minutes over medium flame.

Pour sauce in a baking dish and arrange scaloppine in it.
Bake in preheated 350°F. oven for 10 minutes, turning once.
Spoon sauce over scaloppine and serve.

Serves 6.

Serve with a well-chilled white wine such as Corvo or a good
Verdicchio.

SCALOPPINE ALLA GIARDINIERA
Scaloppine with Garden Vegetables

12 veal scaloppine
½ cup flour
½ cup vegetable oil
2 carrots, scraped, washed, cut lengthwise and then in quarters
½ cup fresh peas, shelled; or ½ package frozen peas, defrosted
    at room temperature
1 16-ounce can artichoke hearts, in brine, drained and cut in
    halves
4 fresh mushrooms, washed and sliced
8 tablespoons butter
½ tablespoon chopped parsley
Pinch thyme
Pinch nutmeg
Salt and freshly ground pepper
½ cup dry white wine
½ cup Brown Sauce (see p. 187)

Dust each veal scaloppine lightly with flour. Heat oil in a large
frying pan until very hot, and brown veal quickly on both sides
in a single layer. Transfer carefully to a warm platter.

Cook carrots in salted water until *al dente* (approximately
8 minutes). If using fresh peas, cook 2 minutes. If using frozen
peas, simply defrost. In 2 tablespoons butter, sauté all vegetables over low flame for 3 minutes. Set aside.

Melt remaining butter in a saucepan and mix in herbs, spices, salt and pepper. Add wine and cook over medium flame until wine evaporates—or about 5-6 minutes. Add brown sauce. Cook 12-15 minutes more.

Combine vegetables with sauce over low flame, cook 2 minutes. Pour layer of sauce into large baking dish, arrange veal scaloppine over it and cover with remaining sauce. Bake 5 minutes in a preheated 350°F oven.

Serves 6.

Serve with a good Chianti.

SCALOPPINE ALLA FRANCESE
Scaloppine French Style

Why this scaloppine was ever named "Francese" I couldn't tell you. However, when properly prepared, it is truly a most delicate and delicious dish.

3 eggs
Salt and white pepper to taste
1 tablespoon heavy cream
1 tablespoon Parmesan cheese
½ tablespoon chopped parsley
12 veal scaloppine
½ cup flour
½ cup vegetable oil
8 tablespoons butter
¼ cup dry white wine
2 lemons (juice of 1½ lemons, and ½ lemon cut into 6 thin slices)
⅓ cup chicken consommé (see p. 42)
Pinch nutmeg

In large mixing bowl, make a smooth batter of the eggs, salt, pepper, cream, cheese and a sprinkle of parsley. Dust each veal scaloppine lightly with flour and soak slices in batter for 1 hour. In a large frying pan, heat oil until very hot. Carefully place scaloppine, 2 or 3 at a time, in pan, and cook quickly until they become crusty and of a golden color. Transfer to a warm platter. Set aside.

Melt the butter in a large baking dish, and arrange the veal scaloppine over the butter. Season with salt and pepper. Add remaining parsley and bake in preheated 350°F oven for 5 minutes. Turn scaloppine, add wine and bake 5 more minutes. Add lemon juice and bake 3 minutes. Add consommé if scaloppine become too dry. Turn again and spoon sauce over all. Place in serving platter. Sprinkle nutmeg over it. Serve with slices of lemon.

Serves 6.

Serve with well-chilled white wine: Soave or Orvieto Secco.

PICCATINA DI VITELLA

12 veal scaloppine
½ cup flour
½ cup vegetable oil
12 tablespoons butter
Salt and white pepper
¼ cup dry white wine
1 tablespoon medium capers
2 lemons (juice of 1½ lemons and ½ lemon cut into 6 thin slices)
½ tablespoon chopped parsley

Dust each veal scaloppine lightly with flour. Heat oil in large frying pan until very hot, and sauté veal quickly on both sides in a single layer. Transfer to a warm platter. Set aside.

Melt butter in a frying pan over low heat. Now cook scaloppine in butter for 5 minutes, turning frequently. They may overlap during this process. Season with salt and pepper. Add wine, and cook until it evaporates—about 4 minutes. Add capers, lemon juice and parsley, and cook another 5 minutes.

Serve each portion with a slice of lemon and some of the pan juices.

Serves 6.

Serve with well-chilled white wine: Soave or Orvieto Secco.

SALTIMBOCCA ALL'EMILIANA

This dish is also called Saltimbocca alla Romana, so, I'm
not certain of its origins. Nevertheless, a flavorful dish of
wonderful appearance and taste.

12 slices veal scaloppine
½ cup flour
½ cup vegetable oil
8 tablespoons butter
Salt and freshly ground pepper
¼ cup Marsala
½ teaspoon sage
½ tablespoon chopped parsley
12 thin, lean slices prosciutto
3 hard-boiled eggs, shelled and cut into wedges
2 pounds fresh leaf spinach, cleaned, stemmed, cooked for exactly
   3 minutes in boiling salted water and drained well, or 2
   packages frozen leaf spinach, defrosted at room temperature,
   squeezed of all water

Dust veal slices with flour. Heat oil in a skillet and quickly
sauté veal on both sides until golden brown. Set aside.

Heat 6 tablespoons butter in large, heavy frying pan. Transfer scaloppine to pan with butter. Season with salt and pepper.
Let butter sizzle, then add wine, and cook for a few minutes,
until wine is slightly reduced. Remove pan from fire. Dust veal
slices lightly with sage and chopped parsley, cover each slice
with a slice of prosciutto, then return pan to fire for another
5 minutes. Place wedges of hard-boiled eggs around veal in pan
to heat through. Remove pan from heat. Meanwhile, heat 2
tablespoons of butter in a skillet, and sauté cooked spinach
until hot. Do not overcook.

Make a bed of hot spinach on a serving platter, lay slices of
veal on it, decorate sides of platter with wedges of egg, then
pour butter and wine sauce over all.

Serves 6.

Serve with a well-chilled Frascati.

VITELLA ALLA GHIOTTONA
Veal "Glutton Style"

From Bologna with love! A dish sure to please a glutton.

½ pound calf's brains, soaked in cold water, cleaned and trimmed
Juice of 1 lemon wedge
½ pound boiled ham in 1 piece
1 cup Italian bread, broken into small pieces
4 pieces dried mushrooms, presoaked (see p. 13), and coarsely chopped
5 fresh mushrooms, coarsely chopped
1 tablespoon chopped parsley
Pinch sage
Pinch thyme
Pinch nutmeg
12 slices veal, about cutlet size, prepared like scaloppine
½ cup flour
3 eggs
¾ cup heavy cream
⅔ cup Parmesan cheese
Salt and freshly ground pepper to taste
¾ cup vegetable oil
8 tablespoons butter
1 teaspoon Dijon mustard
½ cup Marsala
½ cup Brown Sauce (see p. 187)

For the stuffing, blanch brains in salted boiling water and lemon juice for 3 minutes. Drain well and set aside to cool. Cut ham into small cubes. Soak bread in ½ cup cream. When brains have cooled, chop into small pieces. Combine these ingredients with the mushrooms, herbs, spices, and ⅓ cup cheese, and blend well.

Spread 6 slices of veal on work table. Spoon stuffing in equal amounts in the center of each slice. Cover with remaining 6 slices of veal, and press edges together to form a pocket, then seal edges with a meat mallet. Dust lightly with flour.

In a mixing bowl, beat the eggs with ¼ cup cream and ⅓ cup cheese. Salt and pepper to taste. Dip stuffed veal, one by one, in egg batter, coating each heavily. Heat oil in skillet. Cook, one at a time, until crusty and golden, turning once carefully with a spatula. Trim edges of any excess crust, transfer to warm platter. Set aside.

In a frying pan large enough to accommodate all the veal, melt the butter pieces. Add salt and pepper, mustard and wine, and cook until wine evaporates. Add brown sauce, cook 10-15 minutes over low heat. Now place the stuffed veal in the pan, and cook an additional 10 minutes, turning at least once.

Pour hot sauce over veal and serve.

Serves 6.

Serve with a robust red wine, such as Barolo or Gattinara.

COTOLETTA DI VITELLA
ALLA BOLOGNESE
Veal Cutlet Bolognese

This dish is considered the test of a good chef and restaurant.

3 eggs
2 tablespoons heavy cream or milk
½ tablespoon chopped parsley
Pinch nutmeg
2 tablespoons grated Parmesan cheese
Salt and pepper
2 cups plain bread crumbs
6 veal cutlets
1 cup flour
8 tablespoons butter
4 pieces Italian dried mushrooms, presoaked (see p. 13)
6 fresh mushrooms, washed and thickly sliced
2 tablespoons dry white wine
1½ cups Brown Sauce (see p. 187)
1½ cups vegetable oil
6 sage leaves
¼ pound boiled ham, cut into 6 slices
¼ pound fontina cheese, cut into 6 slices

Thoroughly blend the eggs, cream, parsley, nutmeg, Parmesan cheese and salt and pepper and pour into a deep dish. Have the bread crumbs ready in another dish. Dust cutlets with flour and dip into the egg batter and then into the bread crumbs. They should be rather thickly coated. Set aside.

Melt butter in a saucepan and add dried and fresh mushrooms. Cook 6 minutes. Add wine and cook 5 minutes. Add Brown Sauce and cook another 5-6 minutes. Set aside.

Heat oil in a skillet until a bit of batter dropped in it solidifies immediately. Fry cutlets, one or two at a time, until golden brown. Make sure not to let edges burn.

Preheat oven to 350°F.

Place 1 sage leaf (or bit of dried sage) in center of each cutlet. Then cover with slice of ham and top with slice of cheese.

Press down lightly with palm of hand. Pour sauce in baking dish, and arrange cutlets in sauce. Bake until cheese melts evenly over cutlets. Glaze for 3 minutes under broiler. Serve with sauce at the side of each cutlet, not on top.

Serves 6.

Serve with a light red wine: Valpolicella or a Rosatello del Garda.

OSSOBUCO
Veal Shanks

The "bone with a hole"—that's the meaning of ossobuco, which is a Milanese specialty served with their risotto. To complete the delectable experience of eating ossobuco, one must pick the marrow out of the hole in the bone.

6 ossobuco (veal hind shanks) cut into 4-inch pieces
½ cup flour
¾ cup vegetable oil
12 tablespoons butter
¼ teaspoon chopped garlic
4 anchovy filets
8 pieces dried mushrooms, presoaked (see p. 13)
8 fresh mushrooms, washed and sliced
Black pepper
Pinch crushed red pepper
Pinch nutmeg
Pinch ginger
¼ teaspoon sage
2 bay leaves
¼ teaspoon oregano
3 leaves fresh basil, coarsely chopped, or ½ teaspoon dried basil
½ teaspoon rosemary
Pinch thyme
1 tablespoon chopped parsley
1½ cups beef consommé (see p. 42)
1 tablespoon tomato paste
2 cups Brown Sauce (see p. 187)
Rind of ½ lemon, finely chopped
1 cup red wine

Dust ossobuco lightly with flour, and sauté in hot oil until golden. Set aside.

In casserole large enough to hold ossobuco and the sauce, melt the butter and sauté the garlic for 2 or 3 minutes. Add anchovy filets and cook until reduced to a paste. Add the dried mushrooms and cook 3 minutes. Then add the fresh mushrooms and cook another 3 minutes. Stir in all the spices and herbs, and cook 5 minutes, making sure the mixture does not burn or stick to the casserole. If it becomes too thick, add consommé as needed. Blend the tomato paste with ¼ cup hot water, and add to sauce. Cook 3 minutes. Then add the brown sauce and cook 5 minutes.

Arrange ossobuco in casserole, making sure they are covered with sauce. If necessary, add consommé. Cook 10 minutes. Add lemon rind and wine, and cook until wine evaporates, about 10 minutes, basting ossobuco continuously. Cook approximately 30 minutes more. Test with a fork. When done, meat should be tender and almost ready to fall off bone.

Serve with risotto (see p. 92). Oyster forks should be used to scoop out marrow from bones.

Serves 6.

Serve with a big wine: Sfursat from Valtellina or a Barolo.

VITELLO TONNATO
Veal with Tuna Sauce

A truly elegant and flavorful combination of veal and tuna. A perfect summer dish that can be served as an entrée or as a feature of the buffet table.

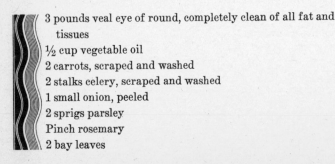

3 pounds veal eye of round, completely clean of all fat and
    tissues
½ cup vegetable oil
2 carrots, scraped and washed
2 stalks celery, scraped and washed
1 small onion, peeled
2 sprigs parsley
Pinch rosemary
2 bay leaves

1 clove garlic, peeled
Salt and pepper
½ cup dry white wine
1½ cups Italian bread, broken up
¾ cup heavy cream
5 anchovy filets
1 large 7-ounce and 1 small 3½-ounce can of Genova or Pastene
     tuna, undrained*
½ tablespoon chopped parsley
1 tablespoon capers
½ tablespoon red wine vinegar
1 cup mayonnaise (see p. 193)

In a roasting pan, combine veal with oil, carrots, celery, onion, parsley sprigs, rosemary, bay leaves, garlic and salt and pepper. Roast in oven preheated to 450°F. for 40 minutes, basting continually. After the first ½ hour, add white wine. When the veal is done, set aside and let cool. Remove vegetables, discarding only the bay leaves and garlic, and put through a grinder. Then blend in food mixer with bread, cream, anchovy filets, tuna, chopped parsley and capers. Add vinegar and mayonnaise and mix thoroughly.

When the veal has cooled, cut into very thin slices. Pour a layer of sauce in a flat glass dish. Arrange veal slices over it and cover with more sauce. Repeat until all the slices are used, ending with a layer of sauce. When completely cool, cover, and allow to rest in refrigerator at least overnight.

I recommend a fresh arugula or arugula and endive salad, or cold fresh asparagus to accompany this dish.

Serves 6.

Serve with a dry white wine, such as Orvieto Secco, well-chilled.

---

* Drain if using American tuna.

FEGATO ALLA FIORENTINA
Calf's Liver Florentine

In the San Frediano district of Florence, they say that a girl is ready for marriage when she faultlessly prepares this dish.

1½ pounds calf's liver, trimmed of all sinews and filmy skin,
   sliced less than a ¼ inch thick (6 slices)
2 eggs
¼ tablespoon chopped parsley
1 tablespoon Parmesan cheese
1 tablespoon heavy cream
Salt and freshly ground pepper
½ cup flour
1 cup plain bread crumbs, sifted
1 pound fresh spinach, well washed, stems removed, or 1 package
   frozen leaf spinach, defrosted at room temperature and well
   drained
8 tablespoons butter
⅓ cup olive oil
2 tablespoons dry white wine
1 lemon cut into 6 wedges

Place liver between sheets of waxed paper, and flatten lightly, taking care not to tear. Combine eggs with parsley, Parmesan cheese, cream and salt and pepper to make a batter. Blend well. Dust liver with flour, dip into batter and then into bread crumbs. Set aside.

If using fresh spinach, cook in salted boiling water for 3 minutes, drain thoroughly. If using frozen spinach, simply defrost and drain. Set aside.

Heat oil over low flame and cook liver, a few slices at a time, making sure to turn often so as not to burn bread crumbs. It should take 3 minutes per slice.

Preheat oven to 350°F.

Melt 6 tablespoons butter in a baking dish, add wine, and cook until wine evaporates—about 1½ minutes. Add liver and bake for 5 minutes in preheated oven. Melt remaining 2 tablespoons of butter in a frying pan, sauté spinach 3 minutes.

Make a bed of spinach on a warm platter and arrange liver on it. Spoon juice from baking dish over liver and spinach, and serve with lemon wedges.

Serves 6.

Serve with chilled white wine, such as Soave or Orvieto Secco.

PICCATINA DI FEGATO
Calf's Liver Piccata

A simple and delicately savory dish from Lucca.

2 pounds calf's liver, trimmed of all sinews and filmy skin,
    sliced ¼ inch thick
Juice of 1 lemon
Salt and freshly ground black pepper
½ cup flour
6 tablespoons butter
1 tablespoon chopped parsley
Pinch rosemary
Pinch sage
Pinch ginger
Pinch nutmeg
1 tablespoon dry white wine

Place the liver between sheets of waxed paper, and flatten lightly, making sure not to tear. Sprinkle a tablespoon of lemon juice and salt and pepper over liver, and set aside for ½ hour.

Dust liver with flour. Melt butter in a large frying pan over low flame and brown liver quickly, turning frequently and carefully. Add herbs, spices, salt and pepper and wine, and cook about 3 minutes. Then add the remaining lemon juice, and cook an additional 2 minutes. Spoon juice over liver and serve.

Serves 6.

Serve with well-chilled white wine—Soave, Orvieto Secco or Verdicchio.

FEGATO ALLA VENEZIANA
Calf's Liver, Venetian Style

Without a doubt, one of the tastiest ways of cooking simple calf's liver and onions.

¼ cup olive oil
2 to 3 large onions, peeled and thinly sliced (enough to make
    3 cups)
10 tablespoons butter
2 pounds calf's liver, sliced ¼ inch thick and then cut into 2-inch
    strips
1 tablespoon dry white wine
½ tablespoon chopped parsley
Salt and freshly ground black pepper
Pinch nutmeg
Pinch sage
2 tablespoons red wine vinegar

Heat oil in a skillet and sauté onion slices to a golden translucence. In a large pan, melt butter and sauté liver over medium flame until lightly browned. Add white wine and cook 3 to 5 minutes. Add parsley, salt, pepper, nutmeg, sage and red wine vinegar. Cook 5 minutes. Then add onions and cook 3 minutes. Serve immediately with onions and pan juices spooned over liver.

Serves 6.

Serve with a light red wine, such as Valpolicella or Barbaresco.

Manzo

Beef

Agnello

Lamb

Maiale

Pork

Selvaggina

Venison

ROLLATINE DI MANZO
Beef Rolls

This succulent dish is a favorite on the Sunday menus of most
families in Liguria.

4–4½ pounds lean beef (preferably eye of round), cut into 12
    ¼-inch slices
Salt and pepper
Pinch nutmeg
Pinch ginger
½ teaspoon sage
1 tablespoon chopped parsley
2 tablespoons grated Parmesan cheese
1½ tablespoons Sultana raisins
1½ tablespoons pignoli
12 slices prosciutto
6 slices fonduta, cut in half
½ cup flour
½ cup vegetable oil
2 cloves garlic, peeled
12 tablespoons butter
6 pieces dried mushrooms, presoaked (see p. 13) and chopped
2 fresh basil leaves, chopped, or generous pinch dried basil
Generous pinch rosemary
2 bay leaves
1 tablespoon tomato paste
½ cup beef or chicken consommé (see p. 42)
1 cup red wine
1 cup Brown Sauce (see p. 187)

Pound beef between sheets of aluminum foil until quite thin.
Sprinkle slices with salt, pepper, nutmeg, ginger, sage, ½
tablespoon parsley and Parmesan cheese. Divide raisins and
nuts evenly among the slices. Place a slice of prosciutto and
½ slice of fonduta cheese on each slice of beef. Then roll beef
around filling and secure with a round toothpick, being sure to
close ends.

Dust rollatine with flour. Heat oil in a frying pan and cook garlic until golden brown. Discard. Sauté rollatine in the same oil for 15 minutes, turning often, and then remove and set aside.

Melt butter in a saucepan and cook mushrooms and remaining herbs over low heat for 10 minutes. Stir in tomato paste and consommé, and cook 5 minutes. Pour this sauce into a baking dish and arrange rollatine in it. Bake in oven preheated to 400°F for 10 minutes, basting often. Then add wine and cook until it evaporates, or about 10 minutes. Add brown sauce and cook an additional 20 minutes, still basting constantly.

Serve with sauce spooned over rollatine, accompanied by braised celery or fennel.

Serves 6.

Serve with Barolo or Sfursat from Valtellina.

MANZO AL BAROLO
Beef Braised in Red Wine

3-pound eye of round beef roast, trimmed of excess fat
2 cloves garlic, peeled and cut in 6 slivers
1½ teaspoons rosemary
1 tablespoon chopped parsley
½ cup olive oil
1 medium onion, peeled
2 carrots, scraped and washed
1 stalk celery, scraped and washed
½ cup dried mushrooms, presoaked (see p. 13)
1 pound fresh mushrooms, washed and sliced
3 fresh basil leaves, chopped, or ½ teaspoon dried basil
3 bay leaves
Pinch nutmeg
Salt and pepper
1½ tablespoons tomato paste
1 cup beef or chicken consommé (see p. 42)
16 tablespoons butter
2 cups Barolo wine (if possible), or any robust Burgundy
1 cup Brown Sauce (see p. 187)

With a sharp knife make 6 incisions in beef, and insert garlic slivers, rosemary and ½ teaspoon chopped parsley in them.

Heat oil in a deep casserole and brown the beef over medium heat for ½ hour, turning frequently to color evenly on all sides. Remove from casserole and set aside.

Put onion, carrots and celery stalk through a grinder. Then cook vegetables in the same casserole for 10 minutes over medium heat. Add dried and fresh mushrooms, remaining herbs, nutmeg, and salt and pepper and cook another 10 minutes. (Add a little consommé, if needed.) Stir in tomato paste and consommé, mixing all ingredients well. Add butter. Once it is melted, replace beef in casserole, cover, and cook 25 minutes, again turning often. Then add wine and cook until wine evaporates, or about 15 to 20 minutes. Add brown sauce and cook another 20 minutes, or until quite tender.

Slice beef and serve with sauce. As an accompaniment, serve a fresh arugula salad, using Trattoria House Dressing (see p. 194) or your own favorite dressing. Manzo al Barolo could also be served with rice or polenta.

Serves 6.

Serve with a full-bodied Grumello or a Chianti Riserva.

STUFATO DI MANZO
Beef Stew

⅓ cup olive oil

12 tablespoons butter

1 teaspoon chopped garlic

1 medium onion, peeled and sliced

2½ pounds lean beef (preferably eye of round) cut in strips
  ½ inch thick, 2 inches long

1 tablespoon chopped parsley

3 fresh basil leaves, chopped, or ½ teaspoon dried basil

Salt and pepper

⅓ teaspoon cayenne pepper

6 carrots, scraped, washed, cut in half and then julienned

3 stalks celery, scraped, washed and diced

2 large red peppers, seeded and cut in strips

½ tablespoon tomato paste

4 cups beef consommé (see p. 42)

1½ pounds potatoes, peeled and cut in chunks

1 tablespoon paprika

Heat oil and butter in a deep casserole, add garlic and onion slices, and cook to a light golden color. Add beef, herbs, salt, pepper and cayenne pepper, and cook 20 minutes, turning beef frequently. Add carrots and celery, and cook 5 minutes. Add peppers, and cook another 5 minutes. Stir in tomato paste and consommé, and bring the whole mixture to a boil. Then add potatoes and paprika. Cook until potatoes are done (20 to 25 minutes). The meat should be tender and the cooking liquid should have reduced by half.

Serves 6.

Serve with a red wine, such as Barbera or Barbaresco.

BOLLITO MISTO
Mixed Boiled Meats

I can hardly think of a more satisfying or tastier dish than a well-prepared Bollito Misto. Although in restaurants you find it as daily fare, it's a holiday dish for most Italians. It is also called Gran Bollito Misto, "grand boiled meats," and it is always served with a vinaigrette sauce or salsa verde.

1½ pounds top round or brisket of beef
Small bunch parsley
Shells of 2 or 3 eggs
1 large tomato, cut in half
6–8 stalks celery, scraped and washed
6–8 white onions, peeled
Salt and pepper to taste
3 chicken legs, each split at joint
1 small veal tongue (the smallest your butcher can give you)
1 medium-sized cotechino (approximately 1 pound)
10–12 small potatoes, peeled and washed
4 carrots, scraped, washed and cut in halves
½ pound string beans, trimmed and washed
1½ cups Salsa Verde (see p. 19)

Add beef, parsley, egg shells, tomato, 1 stalk of celery, 1 onion cut in half, and salt and pepper to 1½ gallons of boiling water.

Cook for ½ hour. Add chicken legs, and cook about 20 minutes. Meanwhile, in separate pot of water, boil tongue and cotechino for about 1½-2 hours. Leave in water.

When beef and chicken are done, remove them and strain broth. Return broth to pot, add rest of onions and the potatoes and cook for 20 minutes. Add carrots. After 5 more minutes, add rest of celery and the string beans. Cook 10 more minutes, but test to be sure that vegetables do not overcook. If done before indicated times, remove vegetables and set aside.

Peel and trim tongue, and cut in ⅛-inch slices. Cut beef in rather thick slices, and cotechino in 1-inch slices. In a baking dish that might also be used as a serving dish, arrange 6 slices of beef, 12 slices of tongue, 6 slices of cotechino and 3 chicken legs and 3 thighs. Cover meat with strained broth and warm in oven preheated to 350°F. for 5 minutes. Arrange vegetables in separate baking dish and cover with 1 cup of broth. Heat in oven for same amount of time.

Before serving, drain all but ½ cup of broth from the meats and all but ⅓ cup from the vegetables. Serve meat and vegetables in separate dishes with *salsa verde* on the side.

Serves 6.

Serve with a red wine, such as a good Gattinara.

ABBACCHIO ALLA ROMANA
Baby Lamb Roman Style

The best abbacchio comes from the Abruzzi region, but the Romans made a cult of it. The tradition of abbacchio is as ancient as the Coliseum.

1 baby lamb, 7–8 pounds, cleaned (head, feet, entrails removed)*
Salt and freshly ground pepper
½ cup olive oil
1 tablespoon chopped parsley

---

* This type of baby lamb is usually found on the market around Easter time. It is not available throughout the year.

3 or 4 twigs rosemary
4 fresh basil leaves, chopped, or ½ teaspoon dried basil
Pinch nutmeg
Pinch ginger
Pinch paprika
Pinch cayenne pepper
5 slices pancetta or lean bacon, chopped coarsely
3 cloves garlic, peeled and cut in halves
10 tablespoons butter
2 bay leaves
1 cup dry red wine

Sprinkle lamb generously with salt and freshly ground pepper, and brush with small amount of olive oil. Then blend the herbs and spices (with the exception of the bay leaves) with the pancetta and 1½ tablespoons of olive oil. Make 6 insertions in lamb with a sharp knife, deep enough to insert 1 piece of garlic and 1 teaspoon of the pancetta herb-and-spice mixture.

Over medium flame, heat remaining oil in a deep, heavy pan large enough to accommodate the lamb. Brown lamb for 20 minutes, turning frequently. Remove lamb and discard oil. Melt butter in pan and add bay leaves. Place lamb back in pan and cook 5 minutes, turning frequently and basting with butter. Add wine, and cook until it evaporates (about 20 minutes), or until lamb is golden and well roasted. Cut lamb in pieces. Serve with sauce spooned over.

Serves 4-6.

Serve with a well-chilled Frascati.

pane
di pasta dura

cotateno
pescellino
roast chicken
and rosemary

worn flowered
tablecloths

white tiled
kitchen —

ochre colums
brown walls
worn shiney
tables

WHITE

VINO FRIZZANTE
Bianco Amabile

ANTONIO ROSSI

The owner of the Tratoria PO
Anton

AGNELLO ALLA BERGAMASCA
Scaloppine of Lamb Bergamasca

The blend of the walnut sauce and the lamb is sensuous bordering on sinful.

½ cup vegetable oil
12 slices of very lean lamb from the leg or eye of round, trimmed
    of all fat and filaments (about 2½–3 pounds)
½ cup flour
8 tablespoons butter
¼ teaspoon chopped garlic
5 ounces peeled walnuts, crushed
1 tablespoon pignoli, crushed
1 teaspoon A-1 Sauce
1 teaspoon Worcestershire Sauce
½ tablespoon chopped parsley
Pinch ginger
Pinch nutmeg
Pinch paprika
Pinch cayenne pepper
Salt and pepper to taste
2 tablespoons heavy cream
½ cup Marsala
½ cup Brown Sauce (see p. 187)

Heat oil in large skillet. Dust lamb scaloppine with flour, and brown quickly in one layer. Transfer to a warm dish.

Melt butter in saucepan; add garlic, cook 3 minutes. Stir in nuts with wooden spoon, making sure that they do not stick to bottom of pan. Add A-1 and Worcestershire sauces; cook and stir for 5 minutes. Add parsley, spices and seasoning. Blend in cream. The sauce should be rather thick at this point. Add Marsala and cook 8 minutes. Add brown sauce, and cook 5 minutes longer. Pour some sauce in large frying pan over medium heat. Add lamb scaloppine, one at a time, and cover each slice with more sauce. Cook 6-8 minutes at most, turning scaloppine to coat well with sauce. Serve with sauce spooned over.

Serves 6.

Serve with a well-chilled Soave Lugana or Rosatello del Garda.

ARISTA DI MAIALE ALLA MAREMMA

Roast Loin of Pork Maremma Style

In my opinion, this is the most succulent, the most savory manner in which to cook pork. The name "alla Maremma" commemorates one of my favorite spots in the Tuscan countryside.

FOR THE PORK:

½ tablespoon chopped parsley
1 teaspoon rosemary
3–4 fresh basil leaves, chopped; or ½ teaspoon dried basil
Pinch oregano
½ teaspoon sage
Salt and freshly ground black pepper
6 slices pancetta or lean bacon, finely chopped
½ cup vegetable oil
3 pounds loin of pork, boned, rolled and tied
3 cloves garlic, peeled and cut in halves
3 bay leaves

Combine herbs, except bay leaves, with salt, pepper, pancetta and 1 tablespoon oil. Mix well. With a sharp knife, make 6 incisions along the side of the loin of pork. Insert a piece of garlic and herb-and-pancetta mixture into each incision. Place pork in a baking dish with remaining oil and bay leaves. Sprinkle with salt and pepper. Roast in preheated 400°F oven for 45 minutes, basting it frequently. If needed, add small amount of water.

FOR THE SAUCE:

8 tablespoons butter
2 shallots, peeled and finely chopped
4 leaves fresh tarragon or tarragon preserved in vinegar, chopped, or ½ teaspoon dried tarragon
½ tablespoon chopped parsley
Pinch nutmeg
Pinch cayenne pepper
Pinch paprika
Salt and freshly ground black pepper
1 teaspoon A-1 Sauce
1 teaspoon Worcestershire Sauce
1½ teaspoons Dijon mustard
½ cup dry white wine
1 cup Marsala wine
1 tablespoon brandy
1 cup Brown Sauce (see p. 187)
½ cup Cream Sauce (see p. 191)

Melt butter in saucepan and cook shallots to a golden brown. Add herbs and spices, and cook 5 minutes. Mix in A-1 and Worcestershire sauces, mustard, the two wines and brandy, and cook until wines have evaporated—about 10 minutes. Then add brown sauce and cook for an additional 10 minutes. Strain sauce through fine wire strainer, return to saucepan, and place over medium heat. Fold in cream sauce and cook 6 minutes. Set aside.

FOR THE PURÉE OF BEANS:

2 cups dried cannellini, presoaked (see p. 000), or fresh cranberry beans, or 2 17-ounce cans cannellini
1½ tablespoons olive oil
Pinch parsley
Pinch sage
Salt and freshly ground black pepper

While pork is roasting, prepare the beans that will accompany it. If using dried beans that have been presoaked, place them in cold salted water and cook for 40 minutes after water comes

to a boil. Follow the same method for fresh beans. Drain and
set aside. If using canned beans, simply drain off liquid.

Heat oil and sauté beans with herbs and salt and pepper for
10 minutes. Then purée beans by putting through a food mill
or in blender. Purée should be at room temperature when served
with the pork.

To serve: When the preceding steps are completed, carve
roast into 12 slices. Reduce oven temperature to 300°F. Pour
a layer of sauce in a baking pan and arrange pork slices over
it. Pour remaining sauce over pork and heat for 5-10 minutes.
Serve with the bean purée.

Serves 6.

Serve with a Chianti Classico Riserva.

BRACIOLE DI MAIALE CON PEPERONATA
Pork Chops with Peppers

This dish always reminds me of country dinners in winter by
the fireplace, served with a robust red wine, like Sfursat from
the Valtellina.

6 loin pork chops, 1¼ inches thick, trimmed of excess fat
½ cup olive oil
2 bay leaves
Generous pinch rosemary
Salt and freshly ground pepper
½ cup dry white wine
2 cloves garlic, peeled
3 anchovy filets, chopped
1 tablespoon chopped parsley
Pinch sage
Pinch oregano
Pinch nutmeg
4 large (red or yellow or green) sweet peppers, seeded and cut
   in strips

Arrange pork chops in baking dish with ¼ cup olive oil, bay
leaves, rosemary and salt and pepper. Bake 45 minutes in oven
preheated to 400°F. After ½ hour, add wine. Baste frequently.

While pork chops are cooking, prepare peppers. Heat ¼ cup oil in a skillet, and cook garlic to a golden brown. Discard garlic; add anchovies, remaining herbs and nutmeg. Then add pepper strips and sauté until tender, without overcooking. This should take 15 minutes at most. Set aside. When chops are done, lower oven temperature to 300°F and mix in peppers with pork chops. Cook additional 5-6 minutes. Spoon cooking juice over chops and serve. Since this is generally considered a winter dish, it should be served with fried polenta (see p. 96).

Serves 6.

SALSICCIE CON FAGIOLI
Sausage with Beans

A savory, filling dish of Tuscan origin served mostly in winter.

2 pounds fresh cranberry beans, 1 pound dried cranberry beans
  or 3 17-ounce cans cannellini
½ cup olive oil
12 links sweet sausage (about 2½ pounds)
Salt and pepper
½ cup dry white wine
1 small onion, peeled and finely sliced
2 cloves garlic, peeled
½ tablespoon chopped parsley
2 fresh basil leaves or ½ teaspoon dried basil
Pinch rosemary
Pinch nutmeg
Pinch crushed red pepper
1 cup Tomato Sauce (see p. 184)
2 tablespoons grated Parmesan cheese

If you are using fresh cranberry beans, place in cold, salted water and cook for 40 minutes after water comes to a boil. If you are using dried beans, soak overnight in water and cook in the same manner. If you are using canned beans, drain the liquid from the beans.

Coat the bottom of a baking pan with 2 tablespoons oil. In an oven preheated to 450°F, bake sausage for approximately 35 minutes, basting with wine. Do not let it become too dry.

To prepare sauce, heat the remaining oil in a large pan. Sauté onion until golden yellow and brown garlic lightly. Discard garlic. Add the beans, herbs and spices. Cook 6 minutes. Add tomato sauce, and cook additional 10 minutes. Set aside.

Drain off liquid from sausage and return to baking pan with the beans. Sprinkle Parmesan cheese on top and bake another 3 to 4 minutes.

Serves 6.

Serve with a full-bodied Chianti.

LUGANEGA CON PISELLI E FUNGHI
Sausage with Peas and Mushrooms

A feature of the Roman menu in the spring, when the inn-keepers begin to serve their clientele *al fresco*. Luganega is a pork sausage the size of your little finger. Since it is not made in links like other sausage but in long strands, the Venetians sell it by the measure instead of the weight.

2 pounds luganega sausage, cut in 3-inch pieces
¼ cup vegetable oil
2 pounds fresh peas, shelled and washed, or 2 packages small
    frozen peas
8 tablespoons butter
4 pieces dried mushrooms, presoaked (see p. 13), and chopped
Salt and pepper
1 pound fresh mushrooms, washed and sliced
½ tablespoon chopped parsley
Pinch nutmeg
Pinch ginger

Fry sausage in oil until nicely browned, approximately 15 minutes. Drain off fat, and set aside.

If you are using fresh peas, cook 3 minutes in salted boiling water. If you are using frozen peas, simply defrost at room temperature. Melt butter in frying pan; add dried mushrooms and salt and pepper to taste. Cook 5 minutes. Add fresh mushrooms, parsley, spices. Cook 10 minutes. Add sausage and peas, and cook additional 5 minutes.

Serves 6.

Serve with a well-chilled Soave or Verdicchio.

ZAMPONE CON LENTICCHIE E FAGIOLI ALLA SALVIA

As mentioned under Ingredients, page 17, zampone di Bologna is not easily obtainable in most cities. However, if you are able to locate an Italian pork store that has it, here's the recipe.

1 cup dry lentils
1 cup dry cranberry beans, or 1½ pounds fresh cranberry beans, shelled
1 3-pound zampone
½ cup olive oil
1 small onion, peeled and finely sliced
2 cloves garlic, peeled
Freshly ground black pepper to taste
½ tablespoon chopped fresh Italian parsley
2 fresh basil leaves
2 pinches rosemary
2 pinches nutmeg
2 pinches crushed red pepper
1 teaspoon fresh sage, finely chopped
¼ cup chicken consommé (see p. 42)

Presoak dried lentils overnight in 2 quarts cold salted water. If you are using dried cranberry beans, presoak overnight in 3 quarts cold salted water.

Wrap zampone tightly in cloth towel, using butcher's twine to secure the wrapping. Place zampone in 2 gallons of cold water, bring to boil, and cook for 2 hours. Remove from pot and unwrap. Set aside.

Drain presoaked lentils, then place in cold salted water and cook for 15 minutes after water comes to a boil. Drain and set aside. Drain presoaked beans, place in cold salted water, cook for 30 minutes after water comes to a boil. Drain and set aside. If you are using fresh beans, cook in same manner as dried presoaked beans.

Divide oil into two ¼ cups and heat in two separate frying pans. Sauté onion (divided into equal portions) in each pan until golden yellow. Add 1 clove garlic to each pan and brown lightly. Discard garlic. Add beans to one pan and lentils to the other. To each pan, add black pepper, parsley (divided equally), 1 basil leaf, 1 pinch rosemary, 1 pinch nutmeg, 1 pinch crushed red pepper, ½ teaspoon fresh sage. Cook over low flame for 10 minutes, mixing frequently.

Slice zampone into 1-inch-thick slices. Pour consommé into large pan. Place zampone slices in consommé with beans on one side and lentils on the other. Cover pan and simmer over low flame for an additional 10 minutes.

Serves 6.

FEGATO DI MAIALE
Pork Liver

A robust-tasting dish of Roman origin. Pork liver prepared this way has a distinctive flavor quite like that of venison.

2 pounds pork liver, trimmed and cut into 12 equal pieces, about
    2 inches long and 1 inch thick
1½ pounds caul fat, cut into 12 pieces, about 3½ x 5 inches
Salt and freshly ground black pepper
1 tablespoon chopped parsley
12 bay leaves
½ cup olive oil
4 tablespoons butter
1 clove garlic, peeled
Juice of ½ lemon
Pinch sage
Pinch rosemary
½ cup dry red wine

Sprinkle caul fat with salt, pepper and parsley. Arrange a bay leaf and a piece of pork liver on each square of caul fat. Roll fat around liver and secure with a round toothpick. Preheat oven to 400°F.

Heat oil and butter in a frying pan, and cook garlic until golden brown. Discard garlic, add liver and sauté liver for 10 minutes, turning constantly. Add lemon juice.

Transfer liver rolls and cooking juices to a baking pan and add herbs, salt, pepper and wine. Bake for 20 minutes, making sure that the liquid does not cook away. Add a little water if necessary.

Serve 2 pieces of liver per portion and spoon juices over them. This dish, usually accompanied by fried polenta (see p. 96), is definitely considered a winter meal.

Serves 6.

Serve with a full-bodied Chianti.

BRACIOLETTE DI SELVAGGINA CON POLENTA AL GORGONZOLA
Small Venison Chops with Polenta and Gorgonzola Cheese

This recipe comes from the savory and rich kitchen of Piedmont and belongs on a fall menu. It is rather expensive and time-consuming, but it is well worth it.

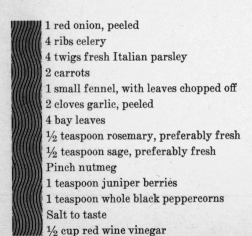

1 red onion, peeled

4 ribs celery

4 twigs fresh Italian parsley

2 carrots

1 small fennel, with leaves chopped off

2 cloves garlic, peeled

4 bay leaves

½ teaspoon rosemary, preferably fresh

½ teaspoon sage, preferably fresh

Pinch nutmeg

1 teaspoon juniper berries

1 teaspoon whole black peppercorns

Salt to taste

½ cup red wine vinegar

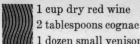 1 cup dry red wine
2 tablespoons cognac
1 dozen small venison chops, cut from the rib

PREPARATION OF MARINADE FOR VENISON:

Cut onion into quarters. Wash and cut ribs of celery in halves and then into strips. Wash parsley and leave whole. Scrape carrots, wash, cut into thick strips. Wash fennel thoroughly, then cut into quarters.

In a deep dish large enough to accommodate venison chops and vegetables, place vegetables, herbs, spices and salt. Add red wine vinegar, wine and cognac. Blend marinade well. Place chops in marinade, basting 5-6 times. Leave at room temperature overnight.

The following day, when ready to cook venison, remove from the marinade and set aside. Also remove the onions, celery, parsley, carrots, fennel and garlic, and pass through food grinder or processor. Set aside. Strain marinade through wire strainer, and set aside.

SAUCE FOR VENISON:

4 thick slices pancetta or bacon
8 tablespoons butter
2 shallots, peeled and finely minced
Pinch ginger
Pinch nutmeg
Pinch paprika
Pinch powdered saffron
½ teaspoon fresh sage, chopped finely
1 teaspoon Dijon mustard
Salt and freshly ground black pepper to taste
½ cup Brown Sauce (see p. 187)

In a large skillet or frying pan, cook pancetta or bacon over medium-high flame for 5 minutes. Place chops in pan, and sauté 20 minutes, turning twice. Remove from fire, and set aside. In baking dish, set over medium heat, melt butter, add shallots, and cook until golden. Add all spices and herbs, and cook 5 minutes, mixing well. Add vegetables from marinade and cook 15 minutes, stirring occasionally. Add brown sauce a bit at a time. Add salt and pepper and mustard and blend well. Cook 3 minutes.

Add strained liquid from marinade, cook 35 minutes. Meanwhile, preheat oven to 350°F.

Remove chops from frying pan, and discard pancetta or bacon and drippings. (Reserve for future use.) Place chops in baking pan with sauce.

At this point, start to prepare Polenta al Gorgonzola (see p. 94). As soon as polenta flour has been poured into the boiling water, place chops in oven, and bake 45 minutes, basting frequently.

When chops are done, Polenta al Gorgonzola should also be ready.

Serve chops with polenta on the side.

Serves 6-8.

Pollami

Poultry

POLLO ALLA TRASTEVERINA
Chicken Trasteverina Style

A robust meal in the peasant style—succulent, and full of flavor. It should be consumed with a well-chilled Frascati wine.

3 small broiler chickens (1½–1¾ pounds each), cut in half, with backbone discarded
8 tablespoons butter
Salt and freshly ground pepper
½ teaspoon chopped garlic
½ tablespoon chopped parsley
½ teaspoon rosemary
¼ teaspoon crushed red pepper
Pinch ginger
3 or 4 pieces dried mushrooms, presoaked (see p. 13), chopped
8 fresh mushrooms, washed and sliced
1 cup dry white wine
½ tablespoon capers
1 18-ounce jar Italian roasted peppers, drained, cut in strips

In two large baking dishes, break up butter into small chunks. Arrange chicken on butter, skin side up, and season with salt and pepper. Sprinkle the garlic over the chicken, bake in oven preheated to 350°F. until butter melts. Baste chicken with butter, add herbs and spices. Bake, basting often, for 10 minutes. Add dried and fresh mushrooms, and cook another 10 minutes, or until chicken is a golden-brown. Add wine, cook 10 minutes. Finally add capers and cook 5 minutes longer.

Place chicken on serving platter, arrange strips of pepper over each piece of chicken, pour hot sauce over, and serve.

Serves 6.

POLLO ALLA VENEZIANA
Chicken Venetian Style

Chicken is such a versatile fowl, and there are innumerable
ways to prepare it. Its meat blends splendidly with the ingredients in this recipe.

3 small broiler chickens (1½–1¾ pounds each), cut in half, with
  backbone discarded
6 tablespoons butter
Salt and freshly ground pepper
¼ teaspoon chopped garlic
4 leaves fresh tarragon, coarsely chopped, or 4 leaves tarragon
  preserved in vinegar
3 leaves fresh basil, coarsely chopped, or ½ teaspoon dried basil
½ tablespoon chopped parsley
Pinch oregano
Pinch thyme
Pinch cayenne pepper
Pinch nutmeg
½ teaspoon black peppercorns
½ cup red wine vinegar
⅓ cup red wine
½ cup dry white wine
1 medium onion, finely sliced
6 slices pancetta or lean bacon, cut in strips

In two large baking dishes, break all but 1½ tablespoons butter
into small chunks. Arrange chickens on butter, skin side up,
and season with salt and pepper. Sprinkle with garlic, and bake
in oven preheated to 350°F. until butter melts. Baste chickens
with butter, add herbs and spices, including the peppercorns.
Bake 20 minutes, basting occasionally, until chickens are golden-
brown. Now pour ¼ cup red wine vinegar over chickens, and
cook 5 minutes. Add red and white wines, and keep basting
chickens for another 15 minutes.

Meanwhile, sauté the sliced onion in 1½ tablespoons of butter
until it becomes translucent. Do not let it brown. Set aside. In
another pan, cook the pancetta or bacon to a light crisp. Mix

pancetta and onion and return to medium heat. Pour remaining vinegar into this mixture, and cook 8 minutes. Add to the sauce in which the chickens are cooking. Stir well. Return chickens to oven for 5 minutes.

Serve the chickens with the sauce spooned over them.

Serves 6.

Serve with a light red wine: Bardolino or Valpolicella.

PETTI DI POLLO ALLA FIORENTINA
Boned Breasts of Chicken Florentine

3 boned breasts of chicken

Salt and freshly ground pepper to taste

Pinch nutmeg

½ pound fresh spinach, washed and chopped coarsely, or ½ package frozen spinach, defrosted at room temperature, squeezed of all water

6 thin slices boiled ham

6 thin slices fontina cheese

2 eggs

1½ tablespoons heavy cream

½ tablespoon chopped parsley

⅓ cup Parmesan cheese

½ cup flour

⅔ cup vegetable oil

8 tablespoons butter

½ cup dry white wine

½ cup Brown Sauce (see p. 187)

Juice of 1 lemon

Skin breasts (skins may be used later for stock); trim of all gristle and fat. Cut breasts in half and butterfly each half (slice each half lengthwise, leaving one side uncut). Place on waxed paper and gently flatten with a meat mallet until pieces are quite thin. Season with salt and pepper and nutmeg.

Steam fresh spinach in ¾ cup salted water for 3 minutes, and drain well. If using frozen spinach, simply drain well when completely defrosted. Place equal amounts of spinach in center of each half of chicken, cover with a slice of ham and a slice of fontina. Close and press down edges of chicken together, then seal edges with meat mallet.

Beat eggs in a mixing bowl, add cream, parsley and Parmesan cheese, and blend well. Dust chicken lightly with flour and dip in egg batter, one piece at a time, making sure to coat heavily. Heat oil in a skillet until very hot, and sauté each piece separately until crisp and golden in color. Trim edges of any excess egg batter, and transfer chicken to a warm platter.

Melt butter in frying pan large enough to accommodate all the chicken. Add wine and cook until it evaporates—about 5 or 6 minutes. Add brown sauce, cook 5 minutes. Then place chicken in the pan, cook 5 minutes. Add lemon juice and cook additional 3 minutes. Turn once. Cook another 5 minutes. Place chicken breasts on serving platter, pour hot sauce over, and serve.

Serves 6.

Serve with a light red wine: Valpolicella or Bardolino.

POLLO ALLA MANDARINA
Chicken Mandarin Style

This combination of chicken and shrimp was a Chinoise-Genovese dish created by Labó's restaurant in Genova at the turn of the century. Chef Labó delighted the palates of the Genovese with his extravagant recipes brought back after a long sojourn in China. Needless to say, his restaurant was a unique place in Genova.

6 small, boned breasts of chicken, trimmed of all fat and gristle
½ cup flour
½ cup vegetable oil
10 tablespoons butter
¼ teaspoon freshly ground black pepper
¼ teaspoon chopped garlic
4 anchovy filets
8 pieces dried mushrooms, presoaked (see p. 13), chopped
Pinch thyme
4 or 5 leaves fresh tarragon, 4 or 5 leaves tarragon preserved in
    vinegar, or ½ teaspoon dried tarragon
½ tablespoon chopped parsley

Pinch oregano
Pinch sage
Pinch ginger
Pinch paprika
Pinch cumin
Package saffron, diluted in ¼ cup hot water
½ cup consommé (see p. 42)
½ tablespoon Dijon mustard
1½ teaspoons A-1 Sauce
1½ teaspoons Worcestershire Sauce
3 drops Tabasco Sauce
½ cup dry white wine
1 cup Brown Sauce (see p. 187)
1 cup heavy cream
1 pound small fresh shrimp, shelled and deveined

Dust chicken lightly with flour. Heat oil until very hot and sauté chicken until golden and very crisp. Set aside.

Melt butter in a saucepan, and add pepper and garlic. Cook 2-3 minutes. Add anchovy filets, and cook until reduced to a paste. Add mushrooms, herbs and spices. Cook 5 minutes, stirring constantly and adding a bit of consommé if needed. Add mustard and a little more consommé, and cook 5 minutes. Add A-1, Worcestershire and Tabasco sauces, and cook another 5 minutes. Keep adding consommé if sauce becomes too thick. Mix in wine and cook until it evaporates—about 5 or 6 minutes. Add brown sauce, and cook 10 minutes. Now strain sauce through a fine wire strainer. Return sauce to saucepan, and warm over medium heat. Fold in heavy cream; mix well with a wire whisk for 2 minutes.

In a large frying pan, combine the chicken and the sauce, and cook 10 minutes, basting chicken with the sauce and adding consommé if necessary. Just before serving, add the shrimp and cook 3 minutes. Divide shrimp evenly over each portion of chicken when serving.

Serves 6.

Serve with a well-chilled Frascati.

POLLO SCARPARIELLA
Chicken "Shoemaker Style"

This crisp, garlicky, aromatic fried chicken is from the *cucina napoletana*.

1¼ cups olive oil
3 small broiler chickens (1½–1¾ pounds each), cut into serving
    pieces, with backbone discarded*
Salt and freshly ground black pepper
1 teaspoon chopped garlic
½ tablespoon chopped parsley
1½ teaspoons rosemary
⅔ cup dry white wine

Heat oil in one very large, or two smaller, skillets until very hot. Season chicken with salt and pepper, and fry over high heat until a golden-brown. This should take no more than 10 minutes. Add garlic, and cook until it becomes golden, being careful not to let it burn. Add parsley and rosemary. Remove pan from heat, and mix in wine. Put back on heat and cook over low heat until wine evaporates (about another 10 minutes). Serve with pan juices poured over chicken.

Serves 6.

Serve with a well-chilled Soave or Verdicchio.

* For a snack, chicken wings alone could be used in this recipe.

POLLASTRINE FARCITE
Stuffed Cornish Game Hens

A dish for "big eaters"—a party dish—as impressive as it is
savory.

4 tablespoons butter
¼ pound boiled ham, diced
3 links sweet sausage (¼ pound), taken out of casing and
    crumbled
3 pieces dried mushrooms, presoaked (see p. 13), chopped
2½ teaspoons chopped parsley
1 tablespoon walnuts, finely chopped
1 tablespoon pignoli, finely chopped
3 fresh basil leaves, chopped, or ½ teaspoon dried basil
1 fresh tarragon leaf, or pinch dried tarragon
Pinch nutmeg
Pinch ginger
½ cup Parmesan cheese
1 cup crumbled white bread soaked in ½ cup cream
6 small fresh Cornish game hens, cleaned thoroughly, with wing
    tips cut off
Salt and freshly ground pepper
½ cup olive oil
2 cloves garlic, peeled
½ teaspoon rosemary
2 bay leaves
¾ cup dry white wine

For the stuffing, melt 3 tablespoons of butter in a skillet over
low flame. Sauté ham, sausage, mushrooms, parsley, nuts, herbs
and spices for 8 minutes, stirring continually so that mixture
does not stick to pan. Set aside to cool. Add cheese and bread.
Blend well.

Rub the rest of the butter inside the cavity and over the skin
of each hen, and season with salt and pepper. Stuff birds, and
truss. Arrange the birds in a roasting pan, breasts up, add oil,
garlic, rosemary and bay leaves. Roast for 20 minutes. Discard

garlic, add wine. Continue to roast and baste birds for another 10 minutes, or until done. Serve with pan juices.

Serves 6.

Serve with a well-chilled Frascati.

PICCIONI AL FORNO
Roast Squabs

Squab is a rather expensive bird on the market, but it is also one of the tastier fowls. This is a simple way to prepare it that leaves the bird its fullest flavor.

6 small squabs (or 3 large squabs) with necks, gizzards,
    wing tips, livers and hearts removed
10 tablespoons butter
6–8 slices pancetta or lean bacon, cut in pieces
½ tablespoon rosemary
½ teaspoon nutmeg
Salt and freshly ground pepper
3 bay leaves
¾ cup Marsala or sweet sherry

Rub ½ of the butter inside the cavities of the birds, add pancetta or bacon, season with rosemary and nutmeg. Truss the birds, season with salt and pepper and place in baking dish with remaining butter and the bay leaves. Roast in oven preheated to 400°F for 15 minutes, basting frequently. Add Marsala, and cook for another 20 minutes, continuing to baste.

Place birds on serving platter,* spoon pan juices over them. Serve with fried zucchini (see p. 174).

Serves 6.

Serve with Gattinara or Ghemme wine.

---

* If using 3 large birds, split each bird in half.

ANITRA ALLA FRUTTA
Duck with Fruit Sauce

An ancient Venetian recipe and a definite departure from the typical French-inspired one. The zest brought to the duck by the various fresh fruits is incomparable. This sauce is as alive as a good wine.

3 ducks (about 4½–5 pounds), prepared for roasting
Salt and freshly ground pepper
2 tablespoons vegetable oil
3½ cups Fresh Fruit Sauce (see p. 192)

Season ducks with salt and pepper, and place in roasting pan with vegetable oil. Preheat oven to 400°F. Place pan in oven, and cook ducks 2 hours, or until brown and crisp. Drain fat 4-5 times during cooking. Set ducks aside and reduce oven to 300°F.

Cut ducks in half, and remove backbones. Also remove the rib cages, being careful not to tear the skin or meat. (This should not present a problem if ducks have been properly cooked.) Then separate the leg and breast, so that each duck is now quartered. Cover bottom of roasting pan with 4 tablespoons of sauce and place ducks in pan. Bake for 10 minutes.

Meanwhile, heat sauce until piping hot. Serve ducks with sauce and fruits spooned over each portion.

Serves 6.

Serve with a red wine, such as a full-bodied Amarone.

Pesce

Fish

BRANZINO AL NATURALE ALLE ALGHE
Striped Bass Baked in Seaweed

In Venice they call this mode of cooking striped bass *la morte reale per il branzino*. ("The royal death for a striped bass.") *Insist* on using the seaweed.

8 tablespoons butter
3 cups chicken consommé (see p. 42)
½ tablespoon chopped parsley
4 leaves tarragon, fresh or preserved in vinegar, chopped
Pinch ginger
3 tablespoons dry white wine
Juice of 1 lemon
Salt and freshly ground pepper
3 pounds fileted striped bass (with heads and tails discarded),
    cut into 6 equal pieces
Small bunch of seaweed, available at fish markets
6 slices lemon

Melt butter in a large baking dish, add consommé, herbs, ginger, wine, lemon juice and seasoning. Arrange the fish in the dish and cover with seaweed. Bake for 15 minutes in oven preheated to 350°F, basting often with the juices. When done, the fish should be completely white and firm.

Remove seaweed and strain the juices through a fine wire strainer. Pour the juices back over the bass, and bake for 2 more minutes. Serve with the juice, and garnish with lemon slices. Serve with braised fennel (see p. 174).

Serves 6.

Serve with a well-chilled Verdicchio or Frascati.

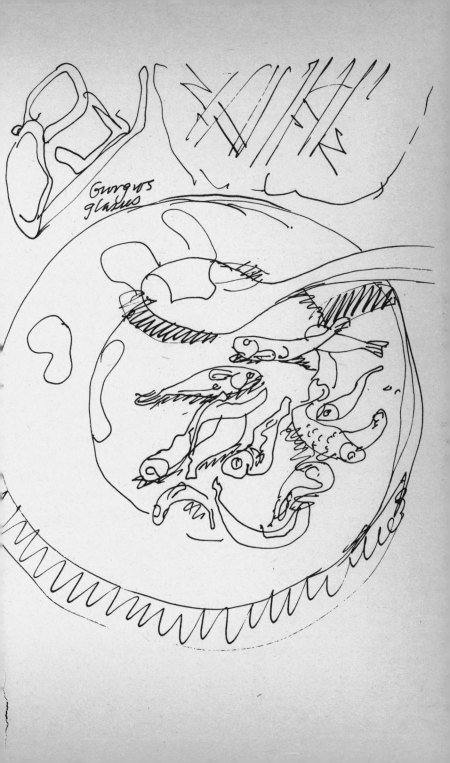

Giorgio's
glasses

BRANZINO FREDDO ALL'AGLIATA
Cold Striped Bass with Garlic Butter Sauce

3 pounds fresh fileted striped bass, cut into 6 pieces
8 tablespoons butter
¼ tablespoon fresh chopped garlic
Pinch ginger
½ lemon
½ tablespoon freshly chopped Italian parsley
Salt and ground white pepper to taste

Preheat oven to 375°F. In a baking pan, melt butter. Place pieces of bass in pan; add garlic, ginger, and the strained juice of lemon. Place pan in preheated oven, cook 8-10 minutes. Add chopped parsley, mix well with butter and juices. Baste fish thoroughly once or twice, cook an additional 3 minutes. Remove from oven, set aside. Allow to cool to room temperature. Serve 1 piece per person; spoon sauce over.
  Serves 6.
  Serve with a well-chilled Frascati.

SOGLIOLA AURORA
Filet of Sole Aurora

The sauce is a variation on the classic Aurora sauce found in many cookbooks, but the stuffing is one of my originals. It is a delicious, delicate main course. Serve with a Castel Chiuro from Valtellina.

6 large slices fresh lemon sole
¾ cup chicken consommé (see p. 42)
½ pound cooked langustine (crayfish) or lobster meat
½ pound fresh mushrooms, washed, roughly broken up
½ cup grated Parmesan cheese
½ tablespoon chopped parsley
4 leaves finely chopped fresh tarragon, or tarragon preserved
  in vinegar
Salt and white pepper to taste
2 tablespoons butter

¾ cup Tomato Sauce (see p. 184)
2 cups Cream Sauce (see p. 191)

Poach sole for about 5 minutes in consommé, adding salt and pepper, if necessary. Let cool.

In mixing bowl, combine langustine meat, mushrooms, cheese, parsley, tarragon and a bit of salt and pepper. Mix well into a coarsely textured stuffing.

Butter a baking pan and spread tomato sauce evenly over the bottom. Drain off consommé and place sole slices in pan. Spoon stuffing onto tops of each slice of sole, and cover with cream sauce. Bake in preheated 350°F oven for 5 minutes, then place pan in broiler for an additional 2-3 minutes (or until cream sauce begins to glaze to a golden-brown). Serve very hot.

Serves 6.

Serve with a well-chilled Soave, Verdicchio or Frascati.

PESCESPADA ALLA MESSINESE
Swordfish Messina Style

Swordfish abounds in the waters surrounding Sicily, and recipes for the fish are very often featured in the kitchens of the island. This particular recipe was given to me by the cook of a small osteria on the beach of Ganzirri, a little village on the Strait of Messina.

2 pounds *fresh* swordfish, cut in 6 equal slices
½ cup flour
¾ cup vegetable oil
12 tablespoons butter
1 large onion, peeled and thinly sliced
1½ tablespoons red wine vinegar
Salt and white pepper to taste
1 tablespoon chopped parsley
Pinch ginger
Pinch nutmeg
½ cup dry white wine

Wash swordfish under cold water and dry well with paper towels. Dust with flour. Heat ½ cup oil until very hot, and fry fish, several slices at a time, 3 minutes for each side. Set aside. Preheat oven to 350°F.

Heat ¼ cup oil with ½ tablespoon butter in a skillet, and sauté onion to a golden, translucent color. Add wine vinegar and let evaporate. Add ¼ teaspoon of salt and a pinch of white pepper, parsley and ginger. Drain off oil and butter, and set onion aside.

Break up remaining butter into chunks in baking dish, add nutmeg and wine, and place in preheated oven. When butter is melted and wine reduced (about 6 minutes), arrange swordfish in dish, and spoon butter over it. Sprinkle with salt and pepper. Cook about 5 minutes. Cover each piece with onion, and cook another 3 minutes. Spoon juices over fish, and serve.

Serves 6.

Serve with a well-chilled white wine, such as Corvo Bianco di Salaparuta.

BACCALA O STOCCAFISSO AL VERDE
Baccala or Stockfish al Verde

Baccala is salt-dried cod; stockfish is cod, haddock or other fish that is dried unsalted. Both require long soaking in several changes of cold water before use: 24 hours for baccala, 4 days for stockfish. The fish can be obtained in Italian markets in dried form, or presoaked and ready for use (both packaged and loose). If baccala is used for this recipe, probably no salt is needed.

The dish, which originated among sailors on long voyages, has been made more sophisticated by the Genovese kitchen.

¾ cup olive oil
½ cup finely chopped parsley
¾ teaspoon chopped garlic
4 anchovy filets chopped coarsely
¼ teaspoon black pepper
2 pounds small potatoes, washed, peeled and cut in ¼-inch slices

4 pounds baccala or stockfish, presoaked, cut in 3-inch chunks
   and drained
½ cup pitted Gaeta olives, chopped
1 tablespoon capers
3 fresh basil leaves, chopped coarsely, or ½ teaspoon dried basil
Salt to taste (if stockfish is used)

Pour ½ of the oil into a baking dish, with a sprinkle of parsley, and the garlic and anchovies. Season with pepper. Make a layer of potatoes on the bottom of the dish, and sprinkle with a little more parsley. Add a layer of baccala, and pour a little oil over it. Sprinkle with parsley, and add some olives, capers and basil. Repeat process until all ingredients are used, ending with a layer of fish, oil, parsley, olives, capers and basil.

Bake for at least ½ hour, or until potatoes are tender but not overcooked.

Serves 6.

Serve with a well-chilled Rosatello or Verdicchio.

GAMBERONI ALLA LUCIANA
Shrimp Luciana

An expensive recipe nowadays because of the high price of shrimp, but well worth the money. Luciana Sauce is another of my former chef Gino's specialties.

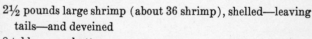

2½ pounds large shrimp (about 36 shrimp), shelled—leaving
   tails—and deveined
8 tablespoons butter
¾ teaspoon chopped garlic
3 filets of anchovies
5 leaves chopped fresh tarragon, or 5 tarragon leaves in vinegar
1 tablespoon chopped parsley
Pinch thyme
Pinch nutmeg
2 leaves fresh basil, chopped, or ½ teaspoon dried basil
Pinch cayenne
Pinch ginger

Pinch turmeric
Freshly ground black pepper (8 mill turns)
1½ teaspoons A-1 Sauce
1½ teaspoons Worcestershire Sauce
3 drops Tabasco Sauce
½ cup dry white wine
2 cups Brown Sauce (see p. 187)
Juice of ½ lemon
3 tablespoons unflavored bread crumbs
½ cup Parmesan cheese

Wash shrimp thoroughly under cold running water, then set aside in refrigerator.

Melt 5 tablespoons of butter in a deep saucepan. Add garlic and sauté until light golden; add anchovies, herbs, spices and bottled sauces, and cook until anchovies have turned to a paste. Add wine and let it reduce, which should take 5 minutes. Add brown sauce and cook 15 minutes, adding some water if it is necessary. Set aside.

Bring to boil a large pot of salted water to which the lemon juice has been added. Drop in shrimp and cook *exactly* 3 minutes. Drain shrimp. Melt remaining butter in a baking pan. Pour ½ of sauce into pan, arrange shrimp in pan, then cover with remaining sauce. Sprinkle bread crumbs, then Parmesan cheese over shrimp and bake in preheated 350°F oven for 10 minutes. Serve 6 shrimp per person.

Serves 6.

Serve with a well-chilled Frascati.

CAPESANTE ALL'UNGHERESE
Scallops Hungarian Style

I was introduced to this dish by an Hungarian friend, an excellent chef, who of course also played the violin rather well—even when insisting on playing it without any clothes on.

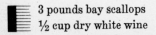

3 pounds bay scallops
½ cup dry white wine

Salt and freshly ground pepper
½ tablespoon chopped parsley
5 tablespoons butter
½ onion, finely sliced
1 teaspoon paprika
Pinch cayenne pepper
Pinch ginger
Pinch turmeric
Pinch cumin
6 pieces dried mushrooms, presoaked (see p. 13), coarsely
   chopped
4 fresh mushrooms, thinly sliced
1 sweet red pepper, cut in thin julienne strips
2½ cups Cream Sauce (see p. 191)
½ cup Parmesan cheese

Wash scallops thoroughly under cold water and drain well.
Place in bowl with wine, sprinkle with salt, pepper and parsley,
and mix well to coat the scallops. Refrigerate for at least 1
hour. Melt butter in a frying pan, and cook onion until a translucent, golden color. Mix in the spices, the dried and fresh mushrooms, and the strips of pepper. Cook 15 minutes. Set aside.

Combine the onion mixture with the cream sauce, cook 5
minutes over low heat.

Drain scallops of liquid and add to sauce. Cook exactly 5
minutes. Serve in soup bowls with Parmesan cheese sprinkled
on top. This dish could also be served with toasted raisin bread.

Serves 6.

Serve with a chilled Rosatello del Garda.

CACCIUCCO ALLA LIVORNESE
Fish Stew, Livorno Style

André Surmain, the cofounder of the Lutèce restaurant in New York, always has Cacciucco when he comes to the Trattoria. He says it is "not as ferocious as bouillabaisse."

1½ pounds boned striped bass, cut into 6 equal pieces (reserving head and tail)

2 pounds whiting, cut into 6 equal pieces (reserving head and tail)

1 pound lemon sole, cut into 6 equal pieces

1 pound small, fresh shrimp, shelled and deveined

1 pound scallops

½ pound additional fish heads and tails

Salt and pepper

½ cup olive oil

½ small onion, finely sliced

¾ teaspoon chopped garlic

1 tablespoon chopped parsley

½ teaspoon oregano

½ teaspoon dried tarragon, or 4 or 5 fresh tarragon leaves, chopped

½ teaspoon dried basil, or 2 fresh basil leaves, chopped

Pinch sage

Pinch thyme

Pinch ginger

Generous pinch crushed red pepper

Pinch cayenne pepper

Pinch paprika

1½ cups Tomato Sauce (see p. 184)

Croutons (see p. 179) (optional)

Wash all the fish thoroughly. Season with salt and pepper and set aside.

In a 4-quart soup pot, heat the oil, and cook onion gently to a translucent golden color. Add garlic, and cook for 5 minutes. Then add parsley, and cook 2 or 3 minutes more. Prepare a bouquet of the herbs and spices in a small bag of cheesecloth.

Put the fish heads and tails into the pot, and add 1½ quarts of hot water. Season with salt and pepper, and immerse the bouquet in the water with one end tied to handle of pot. Bring to a boil, and cook until the stock has reduced to 1 quart, about 25 minutes.

Strain stock carefully through a fine wire strainer lined with two layers of cheesecloth. Then pour it back in the pot, and bring to a boil over medium heat. Add tomato sauce, and bring to boil again. Drain fish of any accumulated liquid, transfer to the pot, and cook between 5 to 8 minutes at the most. The fish should be firm but not overcooked. Serve in soup bowls. Croutons can be added if you like.

Serves 6.

Serve with a red wine, such as a good Barbera.

CIOPPINO DI PESCE

I must confess I tried very hard to attribute the origin of this fish specialty to the kitchen of Italy, certain that I had seen the recipe in the Pellegrino Artusi cookbook. Alas, I have no evidence to dispute its origin among the Italian fishermen of San Francisco. The name *cioppino* has been explained as a distortion of the expression "chip in"—therefore, the chipping in of fish from the day's catch. Whatever its origins, it is a splendid dish.

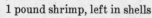

1 pound shrimp, left in shells
3 medium-sized lobster tails*, cut in half and left in shells
3 small, soft shell crabs (in season)
1 medium-sized whiting, reserving head and tail for stock
1 pound fish heads and bones for stock
½ cup olive oil
½ small onion, finely sliced
¾ teaspoon chopped garlic
1 tablespoon chopped parsley

* Fresh lobsters can also be used. You will need 2 of medium size. Each should be split in half lengthwise, and cleaned. Discard the sac near head and the intestinal vein. Detach the claws, and crack.

½ teaspoon oregano
4–5 fresh tarragon leaves, chopped, or ½ teaspoon dried tarragon
3 fresh basil leaves, chopped, or ½ teaspoon dried basil
Pinch sage
Pinch thyme
Pinch ginger
Generous pinch crushed red pepper
Pinch cayenne pepper
Pinch paprika
1½ cups Tomato Sauce (see p. 184)
Croutons (see p. 179) (optional)

Wash all the fish thoroughly. Season with salt and pepper, and set aside.

In a gallon soup pot, heat the oil, and cook onion to a translucent golden color. Add garlic, and cook for 5 minutes. Add parsley, and cook 2-3 minutes. Prepare a bouquet of the herbs and spices in a small bag of cheesecloth. Put the fish heads, tails and bones into pot, and add 1½ quarts of hot water. Season with salt and pepper, and immerse bouquet in water with one end tied to handle of pot. Bring to a boil, and cook until it has reduced to 1 quart. This should not take more than 25 minutes.

Strain stock carefully through a fine wire strainer with 2 layers of cheesecloth in it. Return to pot and bring to a boil over medium flame. Add tomato sauce and bring to boil again. Now transfer all the fish (after draining of any water that might have accumulated) to the pot, and cook 5-8 minutes at the most. Serve in soup bowls, along with croutons, if you like.

Serves 6.

Serve with Barbaresco or Barbera.

Ortaggi

Vegetables

BROCCOLI CON PROSCIUTTO
Broccoli and Prosciutto

3 bunches broccoli, trimmed down to florets and 1 inch of stem,
   washed and drained
Juice and rind of ½ lemon
8 tablespoons butter
¼ cup chicken consommé (see p. 42)
Salt and pepper
¼ teaspoon nutmeg
¾ cup Parmesan cheese
12 thin slices prosciutto

Cook broccoli for 4 minutes in salted boiling water to which the lemon juice and rind have been added. Use wooden spoon to keep broccoli gently pressed down in water. Drain well and run under cold water.

Preheat oven to 400°F. Break up butter into chunks and put in heated baking dish with consommé. When butter has melted, divide broccoli into 6 portions and arrange in baking dish, spooning butter on top. Season with salt and pepper and nutmeg, and cover with Parmesan cheese. Cook 5 minutes in preheated oven. Then lay 2 slices prosciutto over each portion, place in oven again, and cook additional 3 minutes. Spoon butter over the broccoli, and serve.

Serves 6.
Serve with well-chilled Verdicchio.

ASPARAGI CON TUORLI D'OVI
Asparagus with Eggs

2½ pounds rather thin, fresh asparagus, peeled and washed
Juice and rind of ½ lemon
12 tablespoons butter
¼ cup chicken consommé (see p. 42)
Salt and freshly ground black pepper
Pinch nutmeg
Pinch ginger
¾ cup grated Parmesan cheese
1 dozen eggs

Divide asparagus into 6 equal bunches and tie with string.
(Be careful not to bruise tips.) Immerse in boiling, salted water
to which the lemon juice and rind have been added. Cook for
exactly 4 minutes. Drain well, and run under cold water.

Preheat oven to 350°F. Break up 6 tablespoons butter into
chunks in a heated baking dish, and add consommé. When
butter has melted, untie asparagus. Place all 6 portions in dish,
and spoon butter over them. Season with salt, pepper, nutmeg
and ginger. Cover with Parmesan cheese. Bake 5 minutes; remove from oven.

While asparagus is baking, proceed to fry eggs, two at a
time, in the remaining butter. Eggs should be sunny-side up
and not too well done. Transfer carefully to avoid breaking,
and place 2 on each portion of asparagus. Then put back in
oven for another 3 minutes. Spoon butter from baking dish
over the asparagus, and serve.

Serves 6.

Serve with well-chilled Frascati.

CASSEUOLA ALL'EMILIANA
Casserole All'Emiliana

6 medium-sized carrots, scraped, washed and cut in strips
Small bunch celery, scraped, washed and cut into ribs
1 pound fresh string beans, trimmed and washed
6 zucchini, washed
8 tablespoons butter
½ teaspoon chopped garlic
4 anchovy filets
4 tarragon leaves, fresh or preserved in vinegar, chopped
½ tablespoon chopped parsley
Freshly ground pepper to taste
¾ pound boiled ham, cut in strips
1 cup grated Parmesan cheese

Cook carrots in boiling salted water for 10 minutes. Add celery
after 5 minutes and string beans and zucchini after 7 minutes.
Drain well (careful not to bruise vegetables), and run cold

water over them until completely cooled. Cut zucchini lengthwise in strips. Set all vegetables aside.

Preheat oven to 400°F.

Melt butter over low flame in saucepan, and sauté garlic
without browning it. Add anchovies, and cook to a paste. Add
herbs and season with pepper. Spoon small amount of sauce
into a baking dish. Arrange the vegetables and strips of ham
in dish, and pour remaining sauce over. Top with Parmesan
cheese, and bake 10 minutes. Transfer to broiler until cheese
forms a crust.

Serves 6.

Serve with well-chilled Orvieto Secco.

STRONZATA DI VERDURE CON SALSA VERDE
A Mess of Vegetables

The word *stronzata* in the Roman dialect has many connota-
tions, but it is mostly used to mean "a mess," "a pile of this
and that," or "a foolish action." In this case, the name is a
whim of mine. This dish has gained the acclaim of half a dozen
food magazines and is the number-one seller at my restaurants.

1 cotechino (about 1 pound)
1½ pounds fresh asparagus
1½ bunches fresh broccoli, cut into florets with 1-inch stems
1 small head cauliflower, cut into florets, stems and outer leaves
   removed
1 pound fresh string beans, trimmed
¾ cup chicken consommé (see p. 42)
1 cup grated Parmesan cheese
1½ cups Salsa Verde (see p. 191)

Cook cotechino in boiling unsalted water for 1½ hours, prick-
ing it all over with a fork. Set aside.

Wash all vegetables in cold water, then cook in separate pots
of boiling salted water. Cooking times: asparagus, 5 minutes;
broccoli, 4-5 minutes; cauliflower, 10 minutes; string beans, 8

minutes. Carefully drain vegetables and immerse immediately in ice water.

Cut cotechino into 12 slices, ½ inch thick. Put consommé in a large casserole over low heat. Add vegetables, keeping them in separate piles. Sprinkle them generously with grated cheese. Add cotechino slices. Cook slowly, covered, over low heat until vegetables are thoroughly hot. Then place casserole under broiler for about 3 minutes. Sprinkle more Parmesan over vegetables, and serve hot with *salsa verde* on the side. Offer pepper mill.

Serves 6.

Serve with Barbera or Barbaresco.

TORTA DI PATATE
Potato Pie

This dish can be served hot or at room temperature. It is a very good brunch or lunch dish, accompanied by a green salad.

3 pounds large potatoes
4 tablespoons butter
½ cup olive oil
Salt and pepper
1 tablespoon chopped parsley
½ cup Parmesan cheese
½ pound fontina cheese, thinly sliced
¾ pound mortadella, thinly sliced with rind removed

Peel potatoes and slice them lengthwise, ¼ inch thick. Melt butter in a round baking pan and mix in 1 tablespoon of olive oil. Arrange a layer of potatoes in the pan, and sprinkle with salt, pepper, parsley and Parmesan cheese. Cover with slices of fontina and mortadella. Spoon a little oil on top. Repeat the process until all ingredients are used, ending with layer of potatoes. Place in preheated 400°F. oven and bake 25-30 minutes or until tender. Serve by cutting in wedges like pie.

Serves 6.

Serve with well-chilled beer or any light white wine.

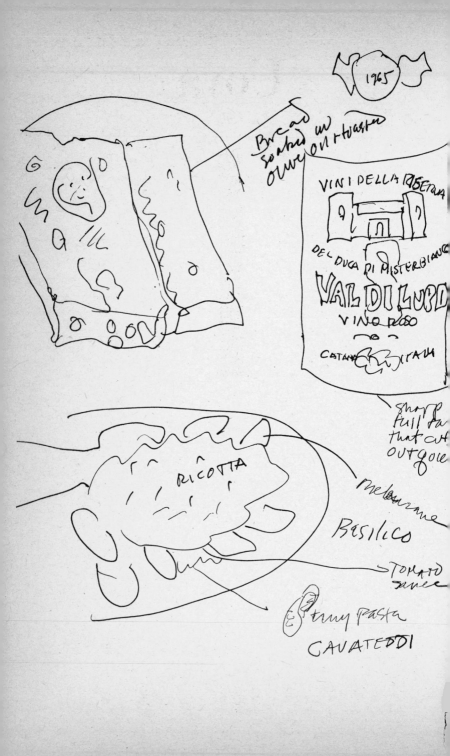

1965

Bread
soaked in
olive oil + water

VINI DELLA RISERVA

DEL DUCA DI MISTERBIANCO

VAL DI LUPO

VINO ROSO

CATANA ITALIA

sharp
full fa
that cut
out goue

melanzane

BASILICO

TOMATO
sauce

tiny pasta
CAVATEDDI

RICOTTA

Uova

Eggs

UOVA ALL'ORIENTALE
Eggs, Oriental Style

These eggs were served in Genova at the turn of the century at the then-renowned restaurant Labó. Its chef-owner, who had lived in China, was bent on impressing his clientele with dishes called by exotic names. His inventive recipes were much sought after.

> 1 pound fresh shrimp
> Juice of ½ lemon and rind
> 12 tablespoons butter
> 2 shallots, peeled and finely chopped
> 1 clove garlic, peeled
> ½ tablespoon shelled walnuts, crushed
> ½ tablespoon chopped parsley
> Pinch ginger
> 1 teaspoon A-1 Sauce
> 1 teaspoon Worcestershire Sauce
> ½ teaspoon Dijon mustard
> 1 dozen eggs
> 1½ tablespoons heavy cream
> 1½ tablespoons grated Parmesan cheese
> Salt and pepper

Place shrimp in cold salted water with lemon juice and rind, and cook 4 minutes after water has come to a boil. Drain and cool. Peel, devein and chop coarsely. Set aside.

Melt 4 tablespoons butter in a skillet, and cook shallots and garlic until golden. Discard garlic; add shrimp, walnuts, parsley, ginger, sauces and mustard. Cook 6 minutes and set aside.

Break eggs in a mixing bowl, and combine with cream and Parmesan cheese. Season with salt and pepper. Scramble with remaining butter to very soft consistency. Fold in shrimp mixture and cook an additional 3 minutes or to your taste. Serve hot with Italian croutons (see p 194). Uova all' Orientale can be served with a salad of sliced cucumbers, scallions and radishes with Trattoria House Dressing (see p. 194) or a dressing of your choice.

Serves 6.

Serve with a well-chilled Orvieto Secco.

EGGS ALLA ROMANA
Eggs Roman Style

A wonderful luncheon dish that is also called Uova Strapazzate
—"scrambled eggs." My good friend Tad Adoue claims that
it is also a dish cooked in his native Texas. He loves to eat it
with a garnish of fresh broccoli sautéed in butter and sprinkled
with Parmesan cheese.

> 1 dozen eggs
> 2 tablespoons heavy cream
> 2 tablespoons grated Parmesan cheese
> Salt and pepper
> 5 tablespoons butter
> ⅔ cup Salas Sarda (see p. 188)

Beat eggs together in mixing bowl. Mix in cream and cheese,
and season with salt and pepper. Melt butter in a skillet, pour
eggs in, and scramble to a very soft consistency. Add the Salsa
Sarda, and cook over very low heat another 5-6 minutes.
  Serves 6.
  Serve with well-chilled beer or light white wine.

Tipico Cucina della Langhe
corso como 6 ☎ 664279
The fantastic riso e barolo
Then a kind of blood pudding
over polenta = The house
Dolcetta = Incredible pink onions
cooked in wine + Bunnett

like a

whole
wheat
flan

GIORGIO
SOAVI
ATE
RABBIT

the
Restaurants
own Dolcetta
8 quite respected
in Milano

Ortaggi e Insalate

Although few Italians are vegetarians, they are lovers of vegetables and salads. More than any other cuisine, except perhaps for the Chinese, Italian cooking abounds with dishes made with fresh vegetables.

Until recent years in Italy, vegetables were used only when in season. The *primizie,* or off-season, hot-house vegetables, were regarded with a certain amount of skepticism; they were thought of as less nutritious, less flavorful and above all much too expensive. I can still remember going into the hills surrounding Savona, my native town, to pick field salad greens to be used for that night's dinner.

The cooking of vegetables is a lot more complicated than it seems. Regrettably, there are few restaurants that really handle vegetables properly. They are usually overcooked. Only the Chinese and occasionally the French know how to cook vegetables just to the *al dente* stage.

FAGIOLINI VERDI DELLA TRATTORIA
String Beans Alla Trattoria

2 pounds string beans, trimmed and washed
8 tablespoons butter
Salt and pepper

Plunge string beans into a large pot of boiling, salted water. Cook for 10 minutes, stirring occasionally with a wooden spoon. When tender but still crisp, drain and rinse immediately under cold running water until completely cooled. Put in refrigerator until ready to prepare for serving.

Sauté in butter, adding salt and pepper to taste. Serve very hot.

Serves 6.

FAGIOLINI VERDI, BROCCOLI E CAVOLFIORI AL BURRO E PARMIGIANO

String Beans, Broccoli and Cauliflower, Butter and Parmesan Cheese

1 pound fresh string beans
1 bunch broccoli
1 small head cauliflower
6 tablespoons butter
½ cup grated Parmesan cheese
Salt and ground white pepper to taste

Cut ends of beans and wash under cold water. Cook in boiling salted water 8 minutes. Drain, cool under cold water, drain, set aside.

Cut thick stems off of broccoli, divide into 6 florets, wash under cold water. Cook in boiling salted water 3 minutes. Drain, cool under cold water, drain and set aside.

Cut leaves off of cauliflower, then cut into 6 florets. Wash well under cold water. Cook in boiling salted water 5 minutes. Drain, cool under cold water, drain again and set aside.

Preheat oven to 375°F. Melt butter in a baking pan. Arrange vegetables in pan, add salt and pepper. Bake 2 minutes. Baste vegetables once or twice with butter sauce. Sprinkle Parmesan cheese over vegetables. Bake 5 more minutes.

Serves 6.

SEDANO AL FORNO

Braised Celery

1 large bunch celery, scraped and well washed
6 tablespoons butter
½ cup chicken consommé (see p. 42)
Salt and pepper
Generous pinch nutmeg
½ cup grated Parmesan cheese

Cut each stalk of celery in 3 sections crosswise. Melt butter in a baking dish, add consommé, and arrange celery in dish. Spoon consommé mixture over celery, season with salt, pepper and nutmeg, and sprinkle with Parmesan cheese. Bake in oven preheated to 400°F. for 20 minutes. Serve as a garnish.

Serves 6.

FINOCCHIO AL FORNO
Braised Fennel

2 large fennel bulbs, trimmed of all tough outer leaves, scraped and washed
6 tablespoons butter
½ cup chicken consommé (see p. 42)
Salt and pepper
Generous pinch ginger
1 tablespoon Pernod
½ cup grated Parmesan cheese

Cut fennel in 6 wedges each. Melt butter in a baking dish, add consommé, and arrange fennel in dish. Spoon some of the consommé mixture over fennel, and season with salt, pepper and ginger. Sprinkle with Pernod and then with Parmesan cheese. Bake in oven preheated to 400°F. for ½ hour or until tender. Serve as a garnish.

Serves 6.

ZUCCHINI FRITTI
Fried Zucchini

8 medium zucchini, washed, and sliced in rounds
Salt and pepper
½ cup vegetable oil
3 tablespoons butter
2 teaspoons chopped parsley

Dry zucchini thoroughly on paper towels, and sprinkle with salt and pepper. Leave for 25 minutes.

Heat vegetable oil in a skillet, and fry zucchini in it until golden brown. Remove and drain again on paper towels. Melt butter in a frying pan and cook zucchini carefully for 3 minutes. Add parsley. Serve hot as a garnish.

Serves 6-8.

FRITTURA DI FUNGHI
Fried Mushrooms

This dish can be used as a garnish or as a snack by itself. It also makes an excellent hot sandwich with Italian bread.

2 pounds extra large mushrooms, 3–4 per pound, washed, dried
    and sliced lengthwise rather thickly
½ cup flour
2 eggs
1 tablespoon milk
½ tablespoon chopped parsley
Pinch nutmeg
Pinch ginger
Salt and pepper
Vegetable oil

Dust mushroom slices with flour. Prepare a batter with eggs, milk, parsley, spices, and salt and pepper. Soak mushrooms in the batter, making sure each slice is well coated. Heat ½ inch of oil in a skillet over high heat, and fry slices of mushroom until dark golden and crisp. Drain on paper towels and serve hot.

Serves 6-8.

MIMOSA DI ARUGULA
Arugula Salad Mimosa

Arugula is a type of "field salad"; its leaves are oblong and smooth, very delicate and tender when the leaves are small. Its taste is slightly bitter. Springtime is when arugula abounds in the Italian greengrocer's shop. In Rome it's called *rughetta* and is believed to have a tonic quality that enhances your appetite. In any case, arugula is a delicacy among green salads. The best dressing for it is olive oil, fresh lemon juice, salt and freshly ground pepper; and a faint touch of fresh chopped garlic is optional.

3 medium bunches arugula
3 tablespoons olive oil
½ lemon
Salt and pepper to taste
The tip of a teaspoon chopped garlic (optional)
2 hard-boiled eggs

Cut off the toughest stems, and wash arugula thoroughly under cold water. Drain very well. Shell cooked eggs, discard the white, mash the yolks finely, set aside. Pour olive oil over salad, and squeeze the ½ lemon on it, making sure to strain the juice. Add salt and pepper and garlic. Toss well, then sprinkle the mashed egg yolks over it.

Serves 6.

NOTE: Arugula leaves will go well with other salad greens. You can also mix arugula and tomato, in which case you follow the recipe above, omitting the hard-boiled eggs and adding 2 ripe tomatoes cut into small chunks. Mix well with same dressing or dressing of your choice.

INSALATA DELLA ZINGARA
Gypsy Salad

This salad can make a perfect meal in itself if served with good crisp bread and a sharp cheese like provolone. It can also be served as an appetizer.

1 small head Boston lettuce, washed, dried and cut
1 small head romaine, washed and dried (use only whiter leaves near the center)
1 bunch watercress, trimmed of any tough stems and washed

1 bunch arugula (when available), washed, or 1 endive, washed
  and sliced
1 small bunch scallions, trimmed of green stems, washed and
  cut in julienne strips
⅔ cup Trattoria Dressing (see p. 194), or your choice
1 cucumber, peeled and sliced
1 bunch red radishes, washed and sliced
2 medium tomatoes (not too ripe), washed and cut in wedges
3 hard-boiled eggs, peeled and quartered
1 7-ounce can Italian tuna, broken into chunks*
½ tablespoon capers
6 anchovy filets
3 pieces pimiento, cut into 12 strips
12 green Spanish olives
12 black olives (preferably Gaeta)
Salt and freshly ground black pepper

Drain all salad greens well, combine in a large bowl, and toss
with ½ cup of dressing. Arrange the remaining ingredients
attractively on the greens, and spoon the rest of the dressing
and the oil from the tuna over the completed salad. Season
with salt and pepper.

Serves 6-8.

---

* Drain if using American tuna.

INSALATA VERDE DEL PASTORE
Green Salad Shepherd's Style

1 small head Boston lettuce
1 small head romaine
1 small head escarole
1 small head chicory
½ bunch watercress
1 cucumber
5 red radishes
4 scallions
¼ cup olive oil
2 tablespoons anchovy paste
Pepper
⅓ cup Trattoria Dressing (see p. 194), or your choice
⅓ cup pecorino cheese, grated

Wash and cut salad greens, using only the inner, tender parts. Trim watercress. Peel and slice the cucumber into thin medallions; trim and slice radishes; julienne the scallions. Drain all thoroughly. Place in a bowl and chill in the refrigerator.

Heat the olive oil gently in a frying pan. Stir in the anchovy paste until well blended, and add pepper to taste. Pour favorite dressing over the salad. Mix well. Sprinkle with cheese, then add the hot anchovy sauce.

Serves 6-8.

INSALATA ALLA CESARE
Caesar Salad

1 small head Boston lettuce
1 small head romaine (use only whiter leaves near center)
1 small bunch escarole (use only whiter leaves near center)
1 bunch watercress, trimmed of tough stems
1 bunch arugula (when available), or 1 endive
1 small bunch scallions, trimmed of green stems, and cut in julienne strips
4½-inch slices Italian bread, or 4 slices plain white bread
¼ cup vegetable oil

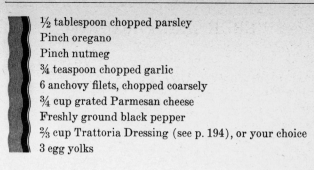

½ tablespoon chopped parsley
Pinch oregano
Pinch nutmeg
¾ teaspoon chopped garlic
6 anchovy filets, chopped coarsely
¾ cup grated Parmesan cheese
Freshly ground black pepper
⅔ cup Trattoria Dressing (see p. 194), or your choice
3 egg yolks

Wash all greens thoroughly. Cut, drain well, refrigerate.

Prepare croutons: Cut bread into small cubes. Heat oil in a skillet, and sauté bread for 3 minutes. Add parsley, oregano, nutmeg and ¼ teaspoon garlic. Turn bread often until golden-brown and rather crisp. By this time, bread should have absorbed all the oil. Sprinkle ¼ cup Parmesan cheese over croutons and mix well. Transfer to paper towels to drain. Arrange greens in salad bowl, add chopped anchovies and remaining garlic, and sprinkle with remaining Parmesan cheese and the pepper. Pour dressing over and toss well. Place croutons on top, mix in egg yolks and once again toss well, until eggs are thoroughly blended.

Serves 6.

INSALATA DI SPINACI
Spinach Salad

This, of course, is not an Italian salad, but since it is very popular at my restaurants, I thought it wrong to omit it from this book.

2 pounds fresh spinach, washed thoroughly at least 3 times,
    trimmed of tough stems, and well dried
¾ pound fresh mushrooms, washed and thinly sliced
½ cup Trattoria Dressing (see p. 194), or your choice
Salt and freshly ground black pepper
2 tablespoons butter
½ pound lean bacon, cut in chunks

Combine spinach and mushrooms in salad bowl. Pour dressing over and mix well. (To achieve best results, mix with your hands.) Season with salt and pepper, mix again. Melt butter in frying pan, and fry bacon to a crisp. Pour bacon fat over salad and top with bacon.

Serves 6-8.

INSALATA DI BROCCOLI
Broccoli Salad

2 bunches broccoli, trimmed down to florets and 1 inch of stem, washed and drained
Juice and rind of ½ lemon
½ cup olive oil
1 tablespoon red wine vinegar
½ tablespoon chopped parsley
5 anchovy filets, finely chopped
½ teaspoon chopped garlic
Freshly ground black pepper
½ teaspoon Dijon mustard

Cook broccoli for 4 minutes in boiling salted water to which the lemon juice and rind have been added. Use a wooden spoon to keep broccoli gently pressed down in water. Drain well and run under cold water. Refrigerate.

To prepare dressing, mix all other ingredients thoroughly in a bowl. Arrange broccoli in bowl, pour dressing over. Toss gently to mix. Let marinate at least 1 hour at room temperature before serving.

Serves 6.

INSALATA DI FAGIOLINI VERDI
String Bean Salad

1½ pounds string beans, trimmed and washed
Juice and rind of ½ lemon
1 small onion, peeled and thinly sliced
¼ teaspoon chopped garlic

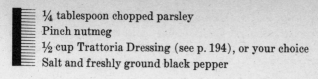

¼ tablespoon chopped parsley
Pinch nutmeg
½ cup Trattoria Dressing (see p. 194), or your choice
Salt and freshly ground black pepper

Cook string beans for 8 minutes, or until *al dente,* in boiling
salted water to which the lemon juice and rind have been added.
Drain well, and cool under cold water. Drain again, and refrigerate until ready to use. Arrange string beans in salad bowl
with onions, garlic, parsley and nutmeg. Pour dressing over,
add salt and pepper, and toss gently to mix. Let marinate at
least ½ hour at room temperature before serving.

Serves 6.

INSALATA DI FAGIOLINI VERDI CON NOCI E CREMA

String Bean Salad with Nuts and Cream

1½ pounds string beans, trimmed, washed, and cut French-style
Juice and rind of ½ lemon
1 tablespoon butter
1½ tablespoons coarsely chopped walnuts
1 pint heavy cream
Pinch nutmeg
Salt and white pepper

Cook beans for 8 minutes, or until *al dente,* in boiling salted
water to which the lemon juice and rind have been added. Drain
well, and cool under cold water. Drain again, and refrigerate.

Melt butter in a saucepan and cook chopped nuts for 5 minutes, stirring continually so they do not stick to bottom of pan.
Add cream and nutmeg, and bring to a boil. Let cool at room
temperature. Add salt and pepper to taste. Then pour over
string beans and mix well.

Serves 6.

INSALATA DI CAVOLFIORI
Cauliflower Salad

1 large cauliflower, trimmed of stem and tough outer leaves,
    washed
Juice of 1½ lemons, and rind of ½ lemon
⅓ cup olive oil
2 teaspoons red wine vinegar
½ tablespoon chopped parsley
½ teaspoon chopped garlic

Cook cauliflower for 10 minutes in boiling salted water to which
the juice and rind of ½ lemon have been added. Drain well and
cool under cold water. Set aside.

To prepare dressing, strain remaining lemon juice and mix
with oil, vinegar, parsley, garlic, salt and pepper. Blend well.

Divide cauliflower into florets. Pour dressing over and toss
gently to mix. Let marinate at room temperature for at least
1 hour before serving.

Serves 6.

INSALATA DI ZUCCHINI
Zucchini Salad

12 medium zucchini
½ cup olive oil
Pinch oregano
2 fresh basil leaves, chopped, or ½ teaspoon dried basil
¼ teaspoon chopped garlic
Juice of 1 lemon
Salt and freshly ground black pepper

Wash zucchini well and cook in 3 quarts of boiling salted water
for 8 minutes. Drain and run under cold water. Refrigerate for
an hour.

Cut zucchini into strips or rounds. Make a dressing with the
olive oil, herbs, garlic, lemon juice, salt and pepper. Toss
zucchini in the dressing, and leave at room temperature for at
least ½ hour before serving.

Serves 6.

Salse e Condimenti

SALSA DI POMODORO
Tomato Sauce

¾ cup olive oil

12 tablespoons butter

2 medium onions, peeled and thinly sliced

½ teaspoon chopped garlic

½ cup Italian parsley, chopped

½ teaspoon oregano

1 teaspoon dried basil, or 5 leaves fresh basil, chopped

½ teaspoon thyme

Salt to taste

½ teaspoon black pepper

1 cup robust dry red wine

4 tablespoons tomato paste

2 cups chicken or beef consommé (see p. 42)

2 35-ounce cans peeled tomatoes (preferably Vitelli), undrained

Heat the oil and butter in a deep 1-gallon pot. When they begin to sizzle, add the onions and chopped garlic and sauté for 5 minutes. Then add the parsley, oregano, basil, thyme, salt and pepper. Sauté until onions become golden. Add the wine and cook 25 minutes, or until wine evaporates.

Dissolve the tomato paste in the stock, add to the onion mixture and cook an additional 10 minutes. Throughout this operation stir the sauce frequently so that it doesn't stick to the bottom of the pot.

Now add the tomatoes and blend thoroughly with the rest of the mixture. Cook 45 minutes. The sauce should be put through a food mill as the final step.

Yield: 2 quarts.

RAGÙ
Meat Sauce

This rich sauce can be served over any pasta. When the sauce is done, the beef*—which is called "stracotto" in Italy—is often served with a fresh salad for luncheon or dinner.

---

* The meat will be very well done.

3 tablespoons olive oil
1½ pounds top round beef in one piece
8 tablespoons butter
½ small onion, peeled and minced
1 clove garlic, peeled
1 tablespoon chopped parsley
Generous pinch nutmeg
½ teaspoon salt
Freshly ground black pepper (10 twists of the mill)
12 pieces dried mushrooms, presoaked (see p. 13), drained and
  chopped
½ cup dry red wine
1 cup tomato paste
4 cups beef consommé (see p. 42)

Heat the oil until hot, and then sauté meat until quite brown.
Set aside.

Melt butter over low flame in a heavy saucepan and sauté
minced onion and garlic, discarding garlic when golden brown.
Add parsley, nutmeg, salt and pepper to onion and cook 5 minutes. Add mushrooms and cook another 5 minutes. Add wine
and let evaporate—about 5-6 minutes. Then add tomato paste
and enough consommé to liquefy it. Cook 10-15 minutes. At this
point, add the meat to the sauce and cook 20 minutes, turning
it often. Add remaining consommé, a little at a time. Cook an
additional 35 minutes. Remove the meat. The end result should
be a rather thick sauce that should have reduced to about 4
cups. Serve with a pasta of your choice.

Yield: 1 quart.

SALSA BOLOGNESE
Meat Sauce Bolognese

2 carrots, scraped and washed
2 stalks celery, scraped and washed
½ medium onion, peeled
¾ cup olive oil
6 tablespoons butter
5 pieces dried mushrooms, presoaked (see p. 13), drained and chopped
½ teaspoon chopped garlic
1 tablespoon chopped parsley
5 fresh basil leaves, chopped, or 1 teaspoon dried basil
Generous pinch thyme
Pinch oregano
Pinch rosemary
2 bay leaves
Pinch nutmeg
½ teaspoon salt
¼ teaspoon freshly ground black pepper
¾ pound chuck beef
¾ pound lean pork
2 cups beef consommé (see p. 42)
1 cup dry red wine
2 cups tomato paste
2 35-ounce cans Italian peeled tomatoes (preferably Vitelli), drained

Put carrots, celery and onion through a food grinder. Heat oil and butter in saucepan. Add vegetables combined with mushrooms, garlic, herbs, nutmeg, and salt and pepper, and cook 10 minutes, continually stirring with a wooden spoon so that mixture does not stick to bottom of pan. Add beef and pork, and cook for 35 minutes, turning often. Add consommé as needed if the mixture becomes too dry.

Add wine and cook until it evaporates—approximately 10 minutes. Then add tomato paste and remaining consommé. Cook 15 minutes, testing meat from time to time to see if it is done. It should be very tender. Add tomatoes and cook 25 minutes more. The mixture should now be quite thick. Remove beef and pork and set aside. Strain sauce through food mill until it has a velvety consistency. Put beef and pork through a grinder and mix into sauce. Blend well over low flame for 5-10 minutes at most. Correct seasoning.

This sauce can be kept refrigerated for approximately a week.

Yield: 1½ quarts.

SALSA BRUNA
Brown Sauce

Brown sauce can be used as a basic sauce for all types of cooking and can be kept refrigerated for at least a month if tightly covered.

2–3 pounds veal bones, cut in small sections
2 pounds beef ribs or any joint bones, cut in small sections
1 pound chicken wings and 1 pound necks
½ cup olive oil
1 teaspoon salt
½ teaspoon freshly ground black pepper
4 bay leaves
3 cloves garlic, peeled
½ tablespoon rosemary
½ cup red wine
16 tablespoons butter
½ tablespoon thyme
2 tablespoons chopped parsley
1 teaspoon dried basil, or 4 leaves fresh basil
½ teaspoon dried tarragon, or 4 or 5 leaves, fresh, or preserved in vinegar
½ teaspoon nutmeg
1½ tablespoons tomato paste diluted in ¼ cup hot water
1 small bunch celery, washed and chopped
5 carrots, washed and chopped in half
1 medium large onion, peeled and chopped in quarters
3 large ripe tomatoes, cut in half
4 envelopes gelatin

Combine veal and beef bones, chicken parts, olive oil, salt and pepper, bay leaves, garlic and rosemary in a large baking dish or roasting pan, and place in oven preheated to 400°F. Cook until bones and chicken are a dark brown color (approximately 1 hour). Watch carefully so that they do not burn. Pour wine over bones, and cook an additional 20-30 minutes, again checking often to avoid burning. Remove from oven and set aside.

In a 3-gallon stockpot, melt butter. Add all remaining herbs and nutmeg, and cook 5 minutes. Add tomato paste and cook 5 more minutes. Now transfer the bones and accumulated juices into the stockpot, being sure to scrape in any little bits of meat from the baking dish. Then add celery, carrots, onions, tomatoes and 1 gallon of warm water. Cook over high heat until water has been reduced by half, continually skimming off the fat that rises to the surface. By this time, the vegetables should be cooked to a pulp. Set stock aside to cool.

Skim again and strain once to remove bones. Then pour through a fine wire strainer lined with a layer of wet cheesecloth. Press down firmly on vegetables to be sure all the juices go into sauce, which should now be caramel in color.* Mix in gelatin and stir well with wire whisk. Refrigerate overnight. It should become the consistency of jellied madrilène.

Yield: 2 quarts.

SALSA SARDA
Sardinian Sauce

This sauce may be used on roast lamb, boiled chicken and beef, and is also excellent on poached fish and Eggs alla Romana (see p. 169). It may be kept refrigerated for one week if tightly covered.

½ cup olive oil
8 tablespoons butter
1 medium onion, finely sliced
½ teaspoon chopped garlic

---

* For a darker brown color, add 2 to 5 tablespoons of Kitchen Bouquet at this time.

8 pieces dried mushrooms, presoaked (see p. 13)
1 tablespoon chopped parsley
Pinch thyme
Pinch oregano
Pinch rosemary
Pinch basil, or 3 fresh basil leaves, chopped
½ teaspoon cayenne pepper
Freshly ground pepper to taste
Pinch nutmeg
Pinch ginger
½ cup dry white wine
1 tablespoon tomato paste diluted in ¼ cup hot water
1 35-ounce can Italian peeled tomatoes, drained
5 anchovy filets, finely chopped
1 tablespoon capers
½ cup Gaeta or Kalamata olives, shaved from pits
1½ teaspoons pignoli

Heat oil and butter in a saucepan over moderate heat. Add onion, and sauté to a deep golden color. Add garlic, and cook 5 minutes. Then add mushrooms, herbs and spices, and cook 5 more minutes, blending well. Add the wine, and cook until it evaporates—approximately 5-6 minutes. Mix in tomato paste and peeled tomatoes, and cook 25 minutes over low heat. Put through a food mill and set aside to cool.

When sauce has cooled to room temperature, blend in anchovies, capers, olives and pignoli.

Yield: 6-8 servings.

PESTO
Fresh Basil Sauce

16 tablespoons butter, cut into little pieces
½ tablespoon finely chopped garlic
Black pepper to taste
1 bunch (or about 3 cups) fresh basil, chopped very, very fine*
¾ cup olive oil
⅓ cup walnuts, chopped
¼ cup pignoli, chopped
¼ pound Parmesan cheese
¼ pound pecorino cheese
¼ cup heavy cream
3 tablespoons cream cheese

Blend all ingredients together either in a food processor, by hand with a wire whisk, or in real Genovese style by grinding down in a mortar with a pestle. Still another way is to put basil, nuts and garlic through a grinder, then combine with other ingredients. Whatever the method, the sauce must become a homogenous, creamy paste.

Leftover sauce, if tightly enclosed in a glass jar and refrigerated, can last one month.

Yield: Approximately 4 cups.

---

* *How to preserve fresh basil leaves:* I would like to share with you my way of preserving fresh basil, which is exactly the way the Genovese have been doing it for centuries. Buy or pluck from your garden as much fresh basil as you can. Cut off the woody stems, leaving the more tender ones attached to the leaves. Wash carefully under a soft spray of cold water. Allow leaves to dry naturally. Take a rectangular container at least 4 inches deep, preferably glass, with an airtight lid (lacking that, devise a cover with a double-duty aluminum foil). Pour 2 cups of good olive oil into the container, add a sprinkling of salt, then a layer of the basil leaves. Repeat the layers of salt and basil until all the basil has been used, making sure when you finish that all the leaves are completely covered with oil. Close the container as tightly as possible, and refrigerate. Whenever you use any of the basil, be careful that the remaining leaves are still covered with oil.

With this method you should be able to preserve your basil supply from the end of August until the middle of March.

SALSA DI CREMA
Cream Sauce

8 tablespoons butter
4 tablespoons flour
Salt and white pepper to taste
Pinch nutmeg
2 cups heavy cream
1 egg yolk, lightly beaten
1½ tablespoons grated Parmesan cheese

Melt butter in a saucepan, add flour, salt and pepper, and nutmeg. Stir with wire whisk until mixture is golden in color. Heat cream in a separate pan and bring almost to a boil. Blend into the butter-and-flour mixture gradually. Cook 10 minutes or until flour can no longer be tasted. Off the flame, quickly blend in the egg yolk. Fold in cheese, blending thoroughly. If sauce seems too thick, add a little heated cream.

Yield: Approximately 2 cups.

SALSA VERDE
Green Sauce

2 hard-boiled eggs, peeled
Large bunch fresh parsley
8 filets anchovies
1 small onion, peeled
2 pieces whole red pimiento
1 tablespoon chopped garlic
1½ tablespoons medium-sized capers
Freshly ground black pepper
¾ cup olive oil
½ cup red wine vinegar

Put eggs, parsley, anchovies, onion and pimiento through grinder; then mix ingredients well in deep bowl, adding garlic, capers and pepper to taste. (This recipe needs no salt.) Still mixing, add oil and vinegar. Taste. Sauce must have a distinctive vinaigrette flavor; if it seems too mild, add more vinegar.

Serve on the side with hot vegetables.

Yield: Approximately 2 cups.

SALSA DI FRUTTA FRESCA
ALLA VENEZIANA
Fresh Fruit Sauce Venetian Style

I use this sauce over roast duck, chicken, squab or other small fowl. If cool when ready for use, it can be poured over the birds and heated in a 350°F oven for 10 minutes.

16 tablespoons butter

1 tablespoon granulated sugar

2 tablespoons red wine vinegar

1 pinch salt

Freshly ground pepper (5 twists of mill)

½ small (7 ounce) jar red or black currant jam

3 lemons (juice and rinds)

3 oranges (juice and rinds)

1 cup sweet Marsala (Florio)

1 tablespoon sultana raisins

5 pitted dried prunes, cut in halves

5 dried apricots, cut in halves

2 cups chicken consommé (see p. 42)

1 apple

2 pears

2 peaches (in season)

1 medium bunch white seedless grapes

½ cup strawberries

½ cup blueberries

10 cherries (in season)

Melt butter in saucepan; add sugar and stir until syrupy. Add vinegar, and cook mixture 10 minutes. Add salt and pepper, then currant jam, and mix well. Add lemon and orange juices and rinds, and let cook for 15 minutes, or until all ingredients are well amalgamated. Then add Marsala and let it reduce, which will take about 6 minutes.

Strain sauce through a fine-mesh strainer. Squeeze the lemon and orange rinds to extract all of their juices, then discard. Return sauce to low fire, add raisins, dried fruits and consommé, and cook 15 minutes.

Meanwhile, prepare fresh fruits: peel apple, pears and peaches, and cut them into wedges about ½ inch thick; wash grapes and separate from stems; clean strawberries and either halve them or leave whole; wash blueberries. Do not pit the cherries, but pull off the stems.

Pour hot sauce into a *bain-marie* or double boiler, and add all fresh fruits. Do not cook. Let sauce stand for about ½ hour.

Yield: 6-8 servings.

SALSA MAIONESE
Mayonnaise

2 cups olive oil
3 egg yolks
½ teaspoon salt
Generous pinch white pepper, or 8 turns of pepper mill
2 tablespoons strained lemon juice, or 1 tablespoon white wine
     vinegar (lemon juice keeps sauce a lighter color)

Warm a mixing bowl with boiling water. Dry thoroughly. Heat oil over low flame until lukewarm.

Place egg yolks in bowl and begin to beat with a wire whisk. Add salt, pepper and a few drops of lemon juice (or vinegar), and continue beating. Then beat in the oil in droplets. By the time you have added 4-5 tablespoons of oil, the sauce will have a heavy, creamy consistency. Gradually add more lemon juice (or vinegar) and continue beating in oil. If it should start to separate, beat one more egg yolk in a separate bowl, then beat the mayonnaise into it a little at a time.

Yield: 2½ cups.

Salsa Maionese alla Russa
Russian Mayonnaise

Follow recipe for Salsa Maionese, and then add the following ingredients:
3 to 4 finely minced fresh tarragon leaves, or a pinch of dried tarragon
2 small packages saffron, soaked in small amount of warm water

Salsa Maionese all'Aglio
Garlic Mayonnaise

Follow recipe for Salsa Maionese, and then add ½ teaspoon finely minced garlic. This type of mayonnaise is excellent served with cold fish.

Salsa Maionese Verde
Green Mayonnaise

Follow recipe for Salsa Maionese, and then add the following ingredients:
3 to 4 finely minced fresh tarragon leaves, or a pinch of dried tarragon
8 fresh spinach leaves, washed and finely minced
1 to 2 finely minced fresh basil leaves, or a generous pinch dried basil

SALSA PER INSALATE DELLA TRATTORIA
Trattoria Dressing

This dressing can be refrigerated for at least a month if kept tightly covered but should be mixed well every time it is used. It is good on any type of salad.

1 quart olive oil
⅔ cup red wine vinegar
1 egg yolk
¾ tablespoon Dijon mustard
1 tablespoon chopped parsley
Generous pinch oregano

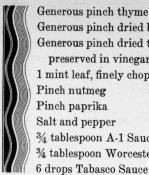

Generous pinch thyme
Generous pinch dried basil, or 4 leaves fresh basil, finely chopped
Generous pinch dried tarragon, or 4 leaves tarragon, fresh or
    preserved in vinegar, finely chopped
1 mint leaf, finely chopped
Pinch nutmeg
Pinch paprika
Salt and pepper
¾ tablespoon A-1 Sauce
¾ tablespoon Worcestershire Sauce
6 drops Tabasco Sauce

Mix oil and vinegar in a large bowl. Using a wire whisk, mix in egg yolk, mustard, herbs, spices and sauces, and beat until dressing has a smooth, velvety consistency. This can also be done in a food processor.

    Yield: Approximately 5 cups.

Dolci

DOLCI/*DESSERTS*

Every Sunday at noon my father would come into the house, carrying a package of pastries or other sweets that he had purchased at Pescetto, the most famous pasticceria (pastry shop) in Savona. That was our Sunday dinner dessert. And hundreds of other fathers were doing the same on Sundays in every town and city in Italy. In the summer, we would have our coffee or granita and gelati (ice creams) or other dessert at one of the many caffé-pasticcerie by the sea or in the Public Gardens. On weekdays, we very seldom had dessert after dinner. When we did, it would generally be fresh fruit, cheeses or, during the winter months, panettone, which was again store-bought. And we never had dessert after lunch, although often in the afternoon we would stop at Pescetto to eat a most delicious pastry along with a cup of espresso or cappuccino. This is pretty much the habit of Italians when it comes to desserts.

There are numerous Italian cakes and pastries, but in order to give you the recipes I would have to steal them from other cookbooks by other authors. Therefore, what follows is a modest list of dessert recipes served in my restaurants, with perhaps one or two other favorites of mine.

ZABAGLIONE CON FRAGOLE*
Zabaglione with Fresh Strawberries

1 pint fresh strawberries
12 yolks of eggs
2½ tablespoons sugar
1 cup sweet sherry or Marsala

Hull the strawberries and wash under cold water. Drain well, and divide among 6 large, stemmed wineglasses. Put egg yolks, sugar and wine into a round-bottomed copper pot** and sprinkle with a little cold water. Place pot over boiling water and proceed to beat mixture rapidly with wire whisk until it turns into a thick, creamy custard. Pour over strawberries and serve.
    Serves 6.

---

* You can, of course, serve Zabaglione unadorned as a dessert.
** You can also use a round-bottomed glass bowl.

ZABAGLIONE FREDDO
Cold Zabaglione

1 pint fresh strawberries or blueberries
1½ cups heavy cream
2½ tablespoons sugar
8 egg yolks
⅔ cup sweet sherry, Marsala, cognac or Grand Marnier
18 ladyfingers (optional)

Clean berries under cold water. Hull the strawberries or remove
the blueberry stems. Drain well and divide among 6 large,
stemmed wineglasses. Refrigerate. Whip the cream, and when
it is nearly thickened add ½ tablespoon sugar, and continue
whipping. Refrigerate. Put the egg yolks, remaining sugar, and
wine, cognac or Grand Marnier into a round-bottomed copper
pot,* and sprinkle with a little cold water. Place over boiling
water, and beat the mixture rapidly with a wire whisk until it
turns into a thick, creamy custard. Place pot over ice, and let
cool before thoroughly blending in the whipped cream. Refrigerate for ½ hour. Pour over the berries. If you are using ladyfingers, arrange 2 or 3 in each glass.
    Serves 6.

BUGIE
"Lies"

This is a tell-tale sweet, which leaves powdery traces of sugar
on the clothing of people who swear they haven't eaten sweets
in years!

3 cups all-purpose flour
¼ cup lard
1½ tablespoons granulated sugar
3 eggs

---

    * In place of a round-bottomed copper pot, you can use a round-bottomed glass
bowl.

3 tablespoons Marsala
½ teaspoon salt
Pinch ginger
Pinch nutmeg
2 cups vegetable oil
Confectioner's sugar

Combine flour, lard, granulated sugar, eggs, Marsala, salt and
spices, and knead into a smooth, soft dough. Put in a bowl,
cover, and let rest 15 minutes.

Cut dough into 3 pieces. Put one piece at a time through a
pasta machine until dough reaches the thickness of 3 sheets of
paper.* Cut into strips 2 inches wide and 10 inches long. Allow
to dry for 15 minutes on a lightly floured work surface. Cut
strips into 3-inch pieces. Make bow ties of every piece by pinch-
ing it in the center.

Heat vegetable oil in a skillet over high heat. Test readiness
of oil with a small piece of discarded dough; it should get
golden-brown rather quickly. Put "bow ties," no more than 6
or 7 at a time, into oil, and fry until golden on both sides.
Transfer to paper toweling to drain for 5 minutes, then sprinkle
liberally with confectioner's sugar. Serve at room temperature.

Serves 6-8 people.

Serve with Asti Spumante.

RAVIOLI DOLCI
Sweet Ravioli

This is a Genovese Christmas dessert.

2 cups all-purpose flour
¼ cup lard
1½ tablespoons granulated sugar
3 eggs
3 tablespoons Marsala

* If you don't own a machine, follow instructions for making pasta by hand
(p. 51).

½ teaspoon salt
Pinch ginger
Pinch nutmeg
Strawberry, peach or cherry preserves, or preserves of your
   choice
2 cups vegetable oil
Confectioner's sugar

Combine flour, lard, granulated sugar, eggs, Marsala, salt, ginger, and nutmeg, and knead into a smooth, soft dough. Put in
a bowl, covered, and let rest at least 15 minutes. Cut dough into
3 pieces. Put one piece at a time through pasta machine until
dough reaches the thickness of 3 sheets of paper.* Cut into
strips 5 inches wide and 10 inches long. Allow to dry for 15
minutes on a lightly floured work surface. Spoon ½-teaspoon
portions of preserves down one side of the dough, about 1¼
inches from the edge and 1 inch apart. Fold the strip in half
lengthwise so that the mounds of preserves are centered and
completely covered. Press down between each mound to seal
the dough well. Then, using a jagged-edged cutting wheel, cut
ravioli into squares, and also trim the outside edges. Put ravioli
on a surface dusted with flour.

Heat vegetable oil in a skillet over high heat. Test readiness
of oil with a small piece of discarded dough; it should get
golden-brown rather quickly. Add ravioli, no more than 5 or 6
at a time, and fry until golden on both sides, turning once.
Transfer to paper toweling to drain for 5 minutes, then sprinkle
liberally with confectioner's sugar. Serve hot or cold.

Serve with Asti Spumante.

---

* If you don't own a machine, follow instructions for making pasta by hand
(p. 51).

MACEDONIA DI FRUTTA FRESCA AL MARSALA

Fresh Fruit Salad with Marsala

½ pound cherries, washed, stems removed, and pitted
¾ pound ripe peaches, peeled and sliced
1 pound grapes, white and red, washed and stems removed
½ pint strawberries, washed and hulled
¼ melon of your choice, cut into balls or cubes
1 large slice watermelon, seeded and cut into balls or cubes
½ cup blueberries, washed and stems removed
⅓ cup sugar
Pinch nutmeg
Pinch ginger
Juice of 2 oranges
Juice of 1 lemon
⅔ cup Marsala, Grand Marnier, or liqueur of your choice
(Depending on the season, other fruits of your liking can be
    added or substituted)

Put all fruits into a large bowl. Add sugar and spices and the
strained juice of the oranges and lemons. Pour liqueur or wine
over. Mix well. Let it marinate for 2 hours before serving,
either refrigerated or at room temperature.

Serves 6-8.

FETTE DI ARANCIE AL LIQUORE E ZUCCHERO

Sliced Oranges with Liqueur and Sugar

6–8 large eating oranges
½ cup Maraschino liqueur, Marsala, Grand Marnier or any other
    liqueur of your choice
3 tablespoons sugar

Peel oranges. Remove all white fibers, slice in rounds, and remove seeds, if any. Arrange slices in a large dish 1½ inches
deep. Pour liqueur or wine over. Sprinkle in sugar evenly. Let
marinate 2 hours, either refrigerated or at room temperature.

Serves 6-8.

Menu Suggestions

When making up a meal you are, naturally, guided by your likes and dislikes, your mood, the season, your guests, the occasion, etc. If inspiration flags, the following menu suggestions should be helpful.

CROSTINI DI ACCIUGHE, MORTADELLA E FONTINA
Hot Anchovy, Mortadella and Fontina Canapés
FUSILLI CON PESTO E PATATE
(½ portion)
Pasta with Pesto and Potatoes
ROSATELLO DEL GARDA
(Light Rosé Wine)

VITELLO TONNATO
Veal with Tuna Sauce
INSALATA DI CAVOLFIORI O BROCCOLI
Cauliflower or Broccoli Salad
CASTEL CHIURO DELLA VALTELLINA
(White Wine)

FREDDO ZABAGLIONE
Cold Zabaglione
ESPRESSO
SAMBUCA

MARINATA DI GAMBERONI E FUNGHI
Marinated Shrimp and Mushrooms
STRACCIATELLA ALLA ROMANA
Roman Egg and Spinach Soup
SOAVE
(White Wine)

OSSOBUCO
Veal Shanks
RISOTTO ALLA MILANESE
Saffron Rice
INSALATA DI ARUGULA
Arugula Salad
GATTINARA
(Red Wine)

RAVIOLI DOLCI
Sweet Ravioli
ASTI SPUMANTE
(Sweet Sparkling Wine)
ESPRESSO

CARCIOFI ALLA ROMANA
Artichokes Roman Style
ZUPPA DI COZZE
Mussel Soup
ORVIETO SECCO
(Dry White Wine)

FEGATO ALLA VENEZIANA
Calf's Liver, Venetian Style
POLENTA FRITTA
Fried Polenta
FAGIOLINI VERDI DELLA TRATTORIA
String Beans Alla Trattoria
CHIANTI RISERVA
(Red Wine)

COMICE PEARS with GORGONZOLA COLOMBO
LIGHT PORT WINE
ESPRESSO

ZUCCHINI RIPIENI DEL GENOVESE
Stuffed Zucchini Genovese Style
FETTUCCELLE ALLA PUTTANESCA
(½ portion)
DOLCETTO DEL GARDA
(Light Red Wine)

VITELLA ALLA GHIOTTONA
Veal Glutton Style
INSALATA DI FAGIOLINI VERDI CON
NOCI E CREMA
String Bean Salad with Nuts and Cream
BAROLO D'ASTI
(Red Wine)

BUGIE
"Lies"
ESPRESSO

CARPACCIO
Pounded Shell Steak
CANNELLONI DI MARE
(1 piece per person)
Cannelloni with seafood filling
FRASCATI
(White Wine)

POLLO ALLA VENEZIANA
Chicken Venetian Style
POLENTA FRITTA
Fried Polenta
INSALATA DI ZUCCHINI
Zucchini Salad
BARBERA D'ASTI
(Red Wine)

MACEDONIA DI FRUTTA FRESCA AL MARSALA
Fresh Fruit Salad with Marsala
ESPRESSO

INSALATA ALLA CESARE
Caesar Salad
PENNE ALLA ZAMPOGNARA
CHIANTI RISERVA DUCALE
(Red Wine)

PICCIONI AL FORNO
Roast Squab
ZUCCHINI FRITTI
Fried Zucchini
ROSATELLO DEL GARDA
(Light Rosé Wine)

FRUTTA FRESCA
Fresh Fruits
Pears, Apples, Grapes
ESPRESSO
COGNAC

VONGOLE OREGANATE DI GAETA
Baked Clams Gaeta Style
ZUPPA DI PASTA E FAGIOLI
Pasta and Bean Soup
VALPOLICELLA
(Red Wine)

STRONZATA DI VERDURE CON SALSA VERDE
A Mess of Vegetables
(Same wine)

FRUTTA E FORMAGGIO
Cheese and Fruit
(Fontina, Grana or Provolone; Pears, Apples or Peaches)
ESPRESSO

CARCIOFI ALLA ROMANA
Artichokes Roman Style
RIGATONI CON ZUCCHINI
(½ portion)
Macaroni with Zucchini
FRASCATI
(White Wine)

SCALOPPINE ALLA FRANCESE
Scaloppine French Style
INSALATA DI SPINACI
Spinach Salad
(Same wine)

FETTE DI ARANCIE AL LIQUORE E ZUCCHERO
Sliced Oranges with Liqueur and Sugar
ESPRESSO

FUNGHI FARCITI DELLA SORA ROSA
Signora Rosa's Stuffed Mushrooms
TORTELLINI DELLA NONNA
(½ portion)
ROSATELLO DEL GARDA
(Light Rosé Wine)

BOLLITO MISTO
Mixed Boiled Meats
GATTINARA
(Red Wine)

GORGONZOLA
(with slices of fresh Italian bread)
ESPRESSO
AMARETTO DI SARONNO

PEPERONI STILE BIFFI
Stuffed Peppers Biffi
PERCIATELLI ALL'AMATRICIANA
(½ portion)
Perciatelli Amatrice Style
BAROLO D'ASTI
(Red Wine)

SOGLIOLA AURORA
Filet of Sole Aurora
SEDANI AL FORNO
Braised Celery
ORVIETO SECCO
(White Wine)

ZABAGLIONE CON FRAGOLE
Zabaglione with Strawberries
ESPRESSO
SAMBUCA MOLINARI

SARDE MARINATE "ALL'AGIADDA"
Marinated Sardines Genovese Style
SPAGHETTINI CARBONARA
(½ portion)
Spaghettini with Bacon, Egg and Cheese
CORVO BIANCO DI SALAPARUTA
(White Wine)

BRANZINO AL NATURALE ALLE ALGHE
Striped Bass Baked in Seaweed
FRITTURA DI FUNGHI
Fried Mushrooms
(Same wine)

BUGIE
"Lies"
MARSALA
ESPRESSO

||||||||||||||||||||||||||||||||||||||||||

MELANZANE RIPIENE
Stuffed Eggplant
TAGLIARINI VERDI AI QUATTRO FORMAGGI
(½ portion)
Green Tagliarini with Four Cheeses
ORVIETO SECCO
(White Wine)

COTOLETTA ALLA BOLOGNESE
Veal Cutlet Bolognese
INSALATA DI BROCCOLI
Broccoli Salad
BARBERA D'ASTI
(Red Wine)

ZABAGLIONE FREDDO
Cold Zabaglione
ESPRESSO

Two Special Menus

On May 9, 1978, I gave the following dinner at the Trattoria da Alfredo to honor my beloved friend James Beard, "Papa of American Cooking." Forty-three of our friends attended this dinner, which was highlighted by one of my waiters making a brief but spectacular appearance as a six-foot-five-inch gorilla (courtesy of Brooks-Van Horn Costume Co.).

MENU

Appetizers:

GAMBERETTI, LUMACHE E CÈPES IN UMIDO
(Baby Shrimp, Snails and Wild French Mushrooms)

ASPARAGI ERBA FREDDI, OLIO E LIMONE
(Cold Grass Asparagus with Olive Oil and Lemon)

FINOCCHIONA E PERE
(Tuscan Salame and Pears)

WINE:
Saran Nature

Pasta:

TAGLIARINI VERDI AL SALTO
WINE:
Rosatello del Garda

Fish:

BRANZINO FREDDO ALL'AGLIATA
(Cold Striped Bass with Garlic Butter Sauce)
WINE:
Frascati

Intermezzo:

MOSCATELLO ROSSO ARGENTINO
(Red Muscatel Grapes from Argentina)

Fowl:

FAGIANO AL FORNO
Roast Pheasant

Vegetable:

FAGIOLINI VERDI, BROCCOLI E CAVOLFIORI
AL BURRO E PARMIGIANO
(String Beans, Broccoli and Cauliflower, Butter and Parmesan Cheese)
WINE:
Gattinara

Desserts:

DACQUOISE MOCHA TORTE
SAVARIN A L'ORANGE
(Pastry Chef: Gino Cofacci*)

CAFFE E LIQUORI
(Espresso and Assorted Liqueurs)

(Wines courtesy of Sam Aaron of Sherry-Lehmann, Inc.)

---

* The dessert recipes, specialties of Mr. Cofacci, are unavailable to me and therefore cannot—*che peccato*—be included.

This menu came about when Ms. Gael Greene called to tell me that she was planning a party for Messieurs Paul Bocuse, Michael Guérard, Roger Vergé and Gaston Lenôtre, who were in New York to perform one of their culinay extravaganzas. Ms. Greene wanted to give the party at the Trattoria da Alfredo and she wanted me to plan the meal and cook it.

Those four *Illuminati* dining at my storefront restaurant? My first impulse was to leave immediately for a long vacation in Siena. I expressed my trepidation, but she held firm: "Who else should cook for them in New York City? And where else should they eat but Trattoria da Alfredo?" And that was that.

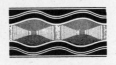

MENU

Appetizers:

CRUDEZZE CON BAGNA CAUDA
(Raw Vegetables with Hot Anchovy Dip)

FRITTATA DI ZUCCHINI, FONTINA E PROSCIUTTO
(Fried Zucchini with Fontina and Prosciutto)

SALUMI ASSORTITI
(A variety of Salami and Cured Hams)

WINE:
Saran Nature

Pasta:

TAGLIARINI BIANCHI AL PESTO
(White Tagliarini with Pesto Sauce)

WINE:
Rosato di Sassella

ZAMPONE CON LENTICCHIE E FAGIOLI ALLA SALVIA
(Zampone with Lentils and Beans Sautéed with Sage)

WINE:
Gattinara

Intermezzo:

FRUTTA FRESCA GELATA
(Cold Fresh Fruit)

Fowl:

PICCIONE AL FORNO ALLA MARSALA
(Roast Squab with Marsala Wine)
WINE:
Ghemme

Intermezzo:

SORBETTO DI AVOCADO ALLA JAMES BEARD
(Avocado Sherbet alla James Beard)

Meat:

**BRACIOLETTE DI SELVAGGINA CON
POLENTA AL GORGONZOLA**
(Small Venison Chops with Polenta and Gorgonzola Cheese)
WINE:
Barolo

Desserts:

**GATEAU PITHIVIERS
DACQUOISE MOCHA TORTE
MILLEFEUILLES**
(Pastry Chef: Gino Cofacci)
WINE:
Cinzano Spumante

CAFFE E LIQUORI
(Espresso and Assorted Liqueurs)

Index

ABOUT THE AUTHOR

ALFREDO VIAZZI was born in Savona, Italy. At the age of eight he became aware of his love for food, a love poorly fed by his mother's meager accomplishments in the kitchen. A few years later, an attractive family friend—and a remarkably good cook —introduced him to the mysteries of sauces and sauciness. The ultimate dream of an Italian boy, according to Viazzi.

Pursuing less homebound interests, Alfredo went to sea for seven and a half years, tried the theater and films, and in 1952 wrote a paperback bestseller, *The Cruel Dawn*. But eventually he was lured by his fascination with food back to the kitchen, and in the mid-fifties he opened his first restaurant, the Portofino, in Greenwich Village. Another restaurant, L'Avventura (a great mis-avventura, as things turned out), prompted the film director Michael Cacoyannis to say: "But Alfredo, you've built a movie set!" Six years later, undaunted and wiser, Viazzi opened the Trattoria da Alfredo and then the Tavola Calda da Alfredo, the two hugely successful restaurants that he still owns and supervises.

Viazzi says: "To run a restaurant is like writing, producing, directing and acting in your own musical, and every night is opening night. What incredible pleasure!"

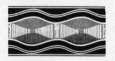